Edition Schott

Charles Louis Hanon
1819 – 1900

The Virtuoso Pianist / Der Klaviervirtuose

60 Exercises / 60 Übungen

For acquiring execution, flexibility, strength and
perfect equality of fingers as well as suppleness of the wrists

Zur Erzielung der Geläufigkeit, Unabhängigkeit, Kraft und
vollkommen gleichmäßigen Ausbildung der
Finger wie auch der Leichtigkeit des Handgelenks

New revised edition / Neu revidierte Ausgabe
after / nach
Alphonse Schotte

ED 22376
ISMN 979-0-001-15935-7

www.schott-music.com

Mainz · London · Berlin · Madrid · New York · Paris · Prague · Tokyo · Toronto
© 2016 SCHOTT MUSIC GmbH & Co. KG, Mainz · Printed in Germany

Contents / Inhalt

Preface

The study of the piano is so universal at the present time, and good pianists are so numerous, that, nowadays, mediocrity on this instrument is not tolerated; the result being that it is necessary to study the piano eight or ten years before attempting to play a piece of moderate difficulty, even before amateurs.

How few people are able to devote so many years to the study of this instrument! It often happens that for want of sufficient practice, the execution is unequal and incorrect; the left hand is impeded by many of the more difficult passages; the 4th and 5th fingers are almost useless for want of special exercises, these fingers being always weaker than the others; and, if the pupil comes across any passages with octaves, shakes or trills, they are executed with difficulty and fatigue; the result being that the rendering is incorrect and lacking in expression.

For some years, we have been seeking to obviate this state of things, by trying to collect in one work special exercises, which will enable the pupils to complete their musical studies in a much shorter time.

To attain this object, it was necessary to solve the following problem: "If the five fingers of each hand were equally practised, they would be able to execute all that has been written for the piano, and the only remaining difficulty would be that of the fingering, which would be easily overcome." The solution of this problem is effected by the work "The Pianist Virtuoso in 60 Exercises".

In this volume are found the exercises necessary for the acquirement of flexibility, strength, perfect independence and equality of the fingers, as well as suppleness of the wrists; all these qualities being necessary for the acquisition of a fine execution: moreover these exercises are calculated to make the left hand as dexterous as the right. Apart from a few exercises, which can also be found in other methods, all works are our own. These studies are interesting and do not tire the student like most 5 finger exercises which are so monotonous that the perseverance and courage of a real lover of music are required to study them.

We have compiled these exercises in such a manner that, after having seen them a few times, it is possible to play them quickly enough to render them an excellent practice for the fingers without it being a loss of time.

If required, all these exercises can be played by different performers, on several pianos at once, which gives emulation to the students and accustoms them to ensemble playing.

In this book are found all sorts of difficulties, so arranged that in every exercise the fingers can rest from the fatigue of the preceding one. The result of this combination is, that without effort or fatigue all the difficulties of execution can be surmounted, and after this exercise a surprising improvement is found.

This work is intended for all students of the piano. As soon as the student has spent one year in study he can use it with much success. As for more advanced pupils, they can master it in a very short time and at its completion will no longer suffer from stiffness in fingers or wrists; this will enable them to overcome the greatest mechanical difficulties. Pianists or teachers who have not had sufficient time to practise, in order to keep up their execution need only to play it for some hours in order to recover the flexibility of their fingers. The whole of this volume can be played in one hour and as soon as it is well understood and practised daily for some time, difficulties will disappear as if by enchantment and the result will be the crisp, light, delicate touch which is the secret of great artists.

To sum up we present this work as supplying a key to all difficulties of execution. We therefore believe that we are rendering a real service to young pianists, to teachers, and to schoolmistresses by proposing that they should adopt for their pupils our work "The Pianist Virtuoso".

[Original wording of the 'only authorized and revised edition'
(English/German) by Alphonse Schotte]

Vorwort

Das Clavierspiel ist in unseren Tagen so verbreitet, die guten Pianisten sind so zahlreich, dass man heutzutage auf diesem Instrument bloße Mittelmäßigkeit nicht mehr erträgt. Es folgt daraus, dass man das Clavier acht oder zehn Jahre gespielt haben muss, ehe man es wagen kann, ein Stück von einiger Schwierigkeit auch nur in einem Kreise von Dilettanten vorzutragen. Wie wenige Personen sind aber in der Lage, so viele Jahre dem Studium dieses Instrumentes zu widmen. Es geschieht daher oft, dass man mangels genügender Arbeit ein ungleichmäßiges und wenig korrektes Spiel hat. Die linke Hand bleibt bei allen etwas schwierigen Figuren hängen, der vierte und fünfte Finger, die immer schwächer als die andren bleiben, hat so gut wie gar keine Kraft, und wenn man einem Oktavenlauf, Tremolo oder Triller begegnet, so bringt man sie meistens nur mit Mühe und Anstrengung zur Ausführung; daher ein wenig sauberes und vollständig ausdrucksloses Spiel.

Während mehrerer Jahre haben wir uns bemüht, in diesem Zustand Wandel zu schaffen, indem wir in einem einzigen Werke diejenigen besonderen Übungen zusammenzufassen suchten, die in viel kürzerer Zeit ein vollkommenes Studium des Clavierspiels ermöglichen.

Um dieses Ziel zu erreichen, war es nötig die Lösung des folgenden Problems zu finden: „Wenn die fünf Finger jeder Hand vollkommen gleichmäßig ausgebildet wären, so würden sie im Stande sein, alles zur Ausführung zu bringen, was für dieses Instrument geschrieben worden ist und man würde alsdann nur noch eine Frage des Fingersatzes vor sich haben, deren Lösung man ohne Schwierigkeit finden würde."

Wir haben dieses Problem durch unser Werk „Der Clavier-Virtuose in 60 Übungen" gelöst. Man findet in diesem Werke die Übungen, die erforderlich sind, um sich Geläufigkeit, Unabhängigkeit, Kraft und vollkommen gleichmäßige Ausbildung der Finger anzueignen, wie auch Leichtigkeit des Handgelenks. Alles Eigenschaften, die zu einem schönen Vortrag unumgänglich sind; außerdem sind diese Übungen darauf berechnet, dass die linke Hand dieselbe Geläufigkeit erwirbt wie die rechte. Von einigen wenigen Übungen abgesehen, die man auch in anderen Schulen antrifft, ist alles Übrige unser eigenes Werk. Die Übungen sind unterhaltend und ermüden den Schüler nicht wie die Mehrzahl der Fünffinger-Übungen, deren Trockenheit so groß ist, dass man die Beharrlichkeit des wahren Künstlers besitzen muss, um den Muth zu haben, sie zu studieren.

Wir haben diese Übungen so zusammengestellt, dass man, nachdem man sie einige Male durchgesehen hat, sie in einem so beschleunigten Tempo spielen kann, dass sie eine ausgezeichnete Arbeit für die Finger sind und man keinen Augenblick verliert, indem man sie studiert.

Man kann, wenn man will, diese Übungen auch auf mehreren Clavieren zugleich spielen, was den Ehrgeiz der Schüler wecken und sie ans Ensemblespiel gewöhnen wird.

Man begegnet in diesem Bande jeder Art von Schwierigkeiten. Wir haben sie in einer Weise geordnet, dass die Finger sich in jeder Übung von der Anstrengung ausruhen, die sie in der vorhergehenden gehabt haben. Es geht aus dieser Anordnung hervor, dass man ohne Anstrengung und Ermüdung alle Schwierigkeiten der Technik zur Ausführung bringt; und nach diesen Übungen gewinnen die Finger eine erstaunliche Leichtigkeit in der Ausführung.

Dieses Werk ist für alle Clavierschüler bestimmt. Wenn man vorher schon ein Jahr studiert hat, so wird man es mit viel Erfolg durcharbeiten. Was die Vorgeschritteneren betrifft, so werden sie es in viel weniger Zeit durchstudieren und alsdann jene Steifigkeit in den Fingern und im Handgelenk, an der sie gelitten, nicht mehr empfinden, in Folge dessen sie fähig sein werden, die größten Schwierigkeiten der Technik zu überwinden.

Die Clavierspieler und die Professoren, die nicht die Muße haben, hinreichend zu üben, um ihr Talent auf derselben Höhe zu erhalten, brauchen es nur einige Stunden lang zu spielen, um die ganze Geläufigkeit der Finger sich wieder anzueignen.

Man kann dieses Werk von Anfang bis zu Ende in einer Stunde durchspielen, und wenn man es vollständig innehat und wiederholt dieses Pensum einige Zeit alle Tage, so verschwinden die Schwierigkeiten wie mit einem Zauberschlage, und man gelangt dahin, jenen schönen, sauberen, freien und perlenden Anschlag zu haben, der das Geheimnis der hervorragenden Künstler ist. Kurzum, wir überreichen dies Werk als den Schlüssel zu allen Schwierigkeiten der Technik. Auch glauben wir den jungen Pianisten einen wahren Dienst zu erweisen, wie auch den Professoren und Pensionslehrern, indem wir ihnen für ihre Schüler den „Clavier-Virtuosen" empfehlen.

[Originalwortlaut aus der „einzig autorisierten und revidierten Ausgabe"
(englisch/deutsch) von Alphonse Schotte]

6

Several variations proposed for the exercise of the rhythm, the strenghtening of the fingers and the suppleness of the wrist, which may be jointed the 35 first exercises.

Die folgenden Anschlagsmöglichkeiten für die ersten 35 Übungen dienen der Festigung des Rhythmusgefühls, der Kräftigung der Finger und der Beweglichkeit des Handgelenks.

First Part

Preparatory exercises for acquiring flexibility, strength, independence and perfect equality of the fingers

For the stretching between the 5th and 4th fingers of the left hand in ascending (A) and between the 5th and 4th fingers of the right hand in descending (B). *

The 20 exercises of this first part should be studied to begin with, at the rate of No. 60 of the metronome to increase gradually to No. 108. The double indication of the movement of the metronome at the beginning of each exercise should be thus understood.

The fingers should be well separated and raised so that each note be heard very distinctly.

Erster Teil

Vorbereitende Übungen für Unabhängigkeit, Kraft und vollständig gleichmäßige Ausbildung der Finger

1

Streckung zwischen dem 5. und 4. Finger der linken Hand beim Aufsteigen (A) und zwischen dem 5. und 4. Finger der rechten Hand beim Absteigen (B). *

Mit dem Zeitmaß 60 des Metronoms werden die 20 Fingerübungen des ersten Teils begonnen, um nach und nach 108 zu erreichen: So ist der Hinweis auf das Zeitmaß zu Beginn jeder Übung zu verstehen.

Damit jede Note so deutlich wie möglich zu hören ist, muss jeder Finger für sich gut angehoben werden.

* As an abridgement we shall for the future only indicate by their numbers the fingers which are to be specially exercised in each lesson. They are shown in parentheses, above bar 1 each (see, for example, the 3rd and 4th fingers on p. 9).

It must be noticed that in the whole of this volume both hands are constantly occupied with the same difficulties: therefore the left hand should become as dexterous as the right. Besides this the same difficulties which are encountered by the left hand in ascending are reproduced by the same fingers of the right hand in descending. This new system of study will cause the hands to acquire the most perfect equality.

* Der Einfachheit halber werden von jetzt an nur diejenigen Fingersätze durch Ziffern angegeben, die in jeder Übung besonders zu beachten sind. Sie stehen in runden Klammern jeweils über dem 1. Takt (s. z.B. auf S. 9 der 3. und 4. Finger).

In diesem Band haben beide Hände dieselben Schwierigkeiten zu überwinden. Auf diese Weise erlangt die linke Hand dieselbe Geschicklichkeit wie die rechte; außerdem müssen die durch die linke Hand im Aufsteigen zu überwindenden Schwierigkeiten von denselben Fingern der rechten Hand im Absteigen bewältigt werden. Diese neue Art von Fingerübungen führt zur vollkommen gleichmäßigen Ausbildung beider Hände.

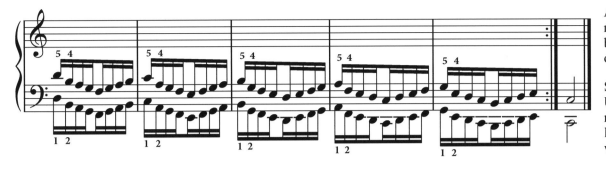

As soon as this exercise is mastered, the second should be studied without stopping on this note.

Sobald man diese erste Übung beherrscht, studiert man die zweite, ohne die letzte Note über ihren Zeitwert hinaus zu verlängern.

2

As soon as this exercise is fully mastered, the preceding one and this one should be recommenced and played four times without interruption. By thus studying these and the following exercises, the fingers shall be considerably strengthened.

Sobald die Finger diese Übung einwandfrei beherrschen, wird die vorhergehende sowie diese 4-mal ohne Unterbrechung durchgespielt, ebenso die nachfolgenden Übungen. Dabei werden sich die Finger in bemerkenswerter Weise kräftigen.

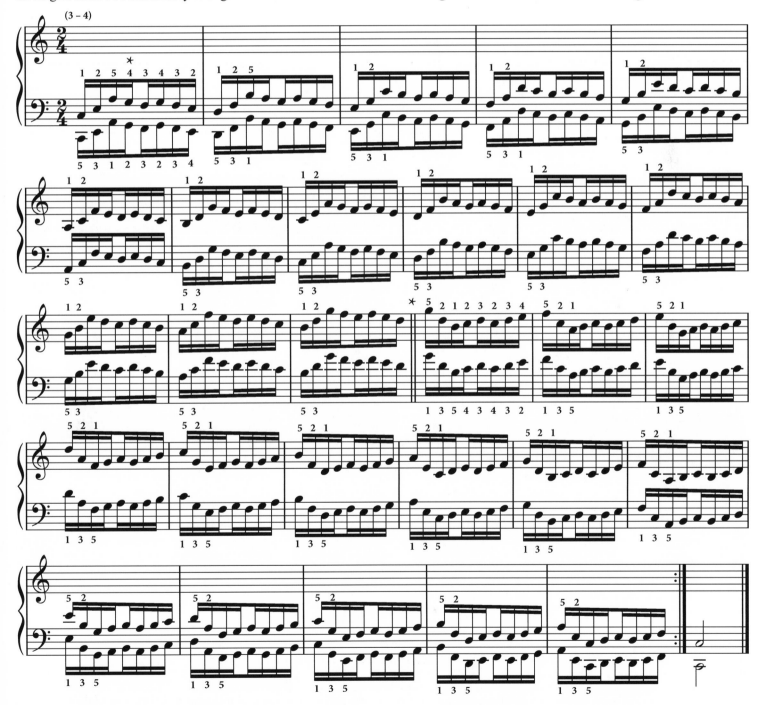

* As the 4th and 5th fingers are naturally weak it should be noticed, that this exercise, and the following up to No. 31 are composed in order to make them as strong as the 2nd and 3rd fingers.

* 4. und 5. Finger sind von Natur aus eher schwach. So haben diese und die folgenden Übungen bis No. 31 den Zweck, sie ebenso stark und geläufig zu machen wie den 2. und 3. Finger.

3

Before beginning to study this No. 3 the two preceding exercises should be played twice without stopping. As soon as No. 3 is well mastered, No. 4 should be studied, then No. 5, and as soon as they are perfectly mastered, they should all three be played at least four times without interruption, so as not to stop until the last note of page 12. All these exercises should be studied in the same way; therefore, in this first part, stops should be made only on the last note of pages 9, 12, 15, 18, 21, 24, and 27.

Wie bereits empfohlen, sollen die beiden vorangehenden Übungen ohne innezuhalten durchgespielt werden. Erst dann folgt No. 3 und sobald diese einwandfrei beherrscht wird, folgen die Nos. 4 und 5. Alle drei Übungen sind ohne Unterbrechung mindestens 4-mal durchzuspielen, mit Innehalten beim letzten Mal auf der Schlussnote von S. 12. Bei diesen Übungen wird also immer erst auf der letzten Note der Seiten 9, 12, 15, 18, 21, 24 und 27 aufgehört.

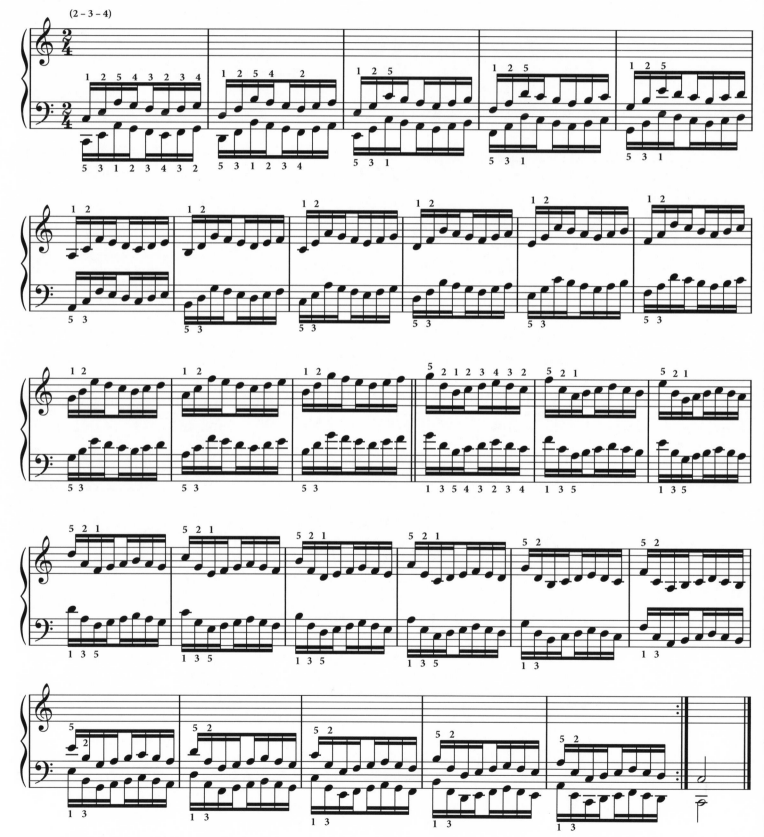

4

A special exercise for the 3rd, 4th and 5th fingers of the left hand.

Sonderübung für den 3., 4. und 5. Finger der linken Hand.

5

We think it wise to repeat that it is necessary to raise and lower the fingers precisely in these exercises, until the whole of this volume is perfectly mastered.

Es muss immer wieder darauf hingewiesen werden, wie wichtig es ist, die Finger sauber zu heben und zu senken, damit alle Töne deutlich artikuliert werden. Das gilt für alle Übungen dieses Bandes.

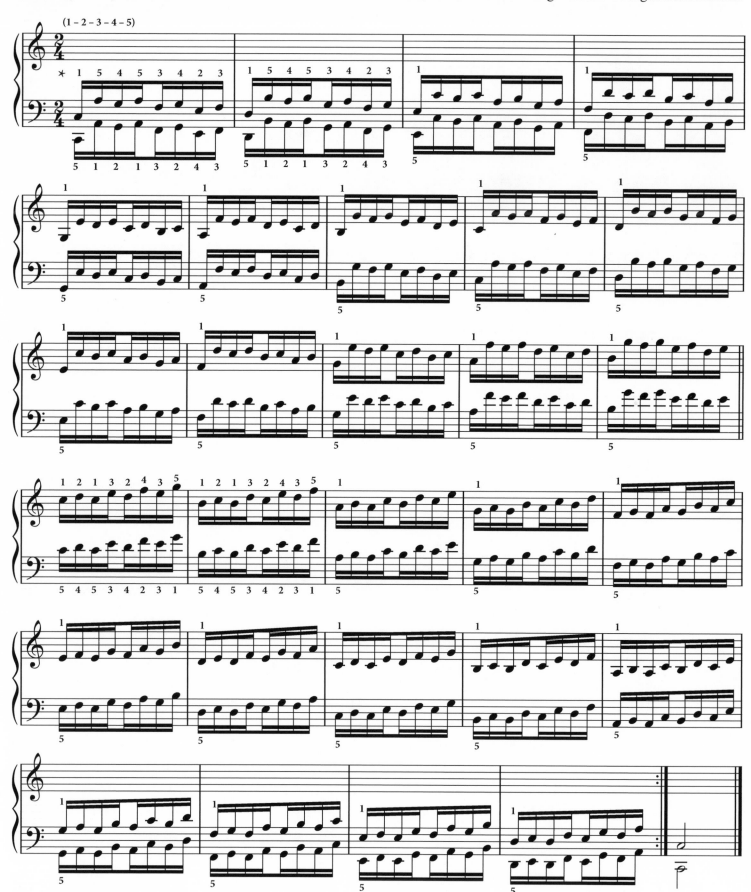

* Preparatory lesson for the trill, with the 4th and 5th fingers of the right hand.

* Vorübung zum Triller für den 4. und 5. Finger der rechten Hand.

6

In order to attain good results it is indispensable to play at least once a day the exercises which have already been learnt.

Um gute Resultate zu erzielen, ist es unumgänglich, die erarbeiteten Etüden täglich wenigstens einmal zu spielen.

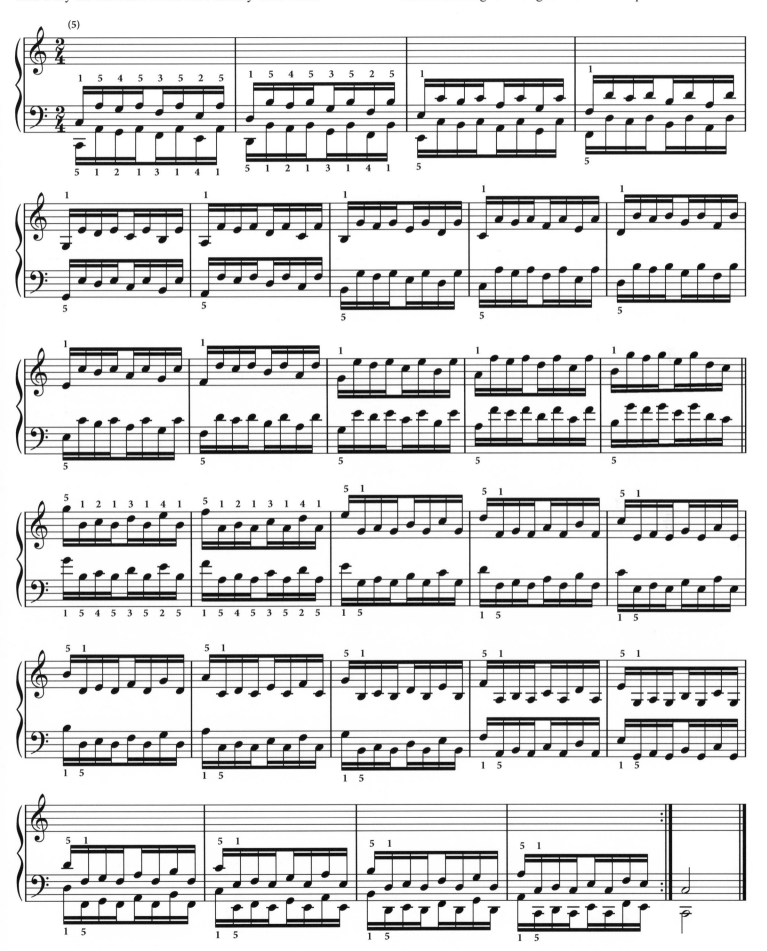

7

This exercise is of the greatest importance for the 3rd, 4th and 5th fingers.

Übung von höchster Wichtigkeit für den 3., 4. und 5. Finger.

8

This exercise is very important for all five fingers.

Übung von gleicher Wichtigkeit für alle 5 Finger.

9

Stretching between the 4th and 5th fingers, and training of all five fingers.

Streckung zwischen dem 4. und 5. Finger und Training aller 5 Finger.

10

Preparatory lesson for the trill with the 3rd and 4th fingers of the left hand in ascending (A) and the 3rd and 4th fingers of the right hand in descending (B).

Vorübung zum Triller für den 3. und 4. Finger der linken Hand im Aufsteigen (A) und für den 3. und 4. Finger der rechten Hand im Absteigen (B).

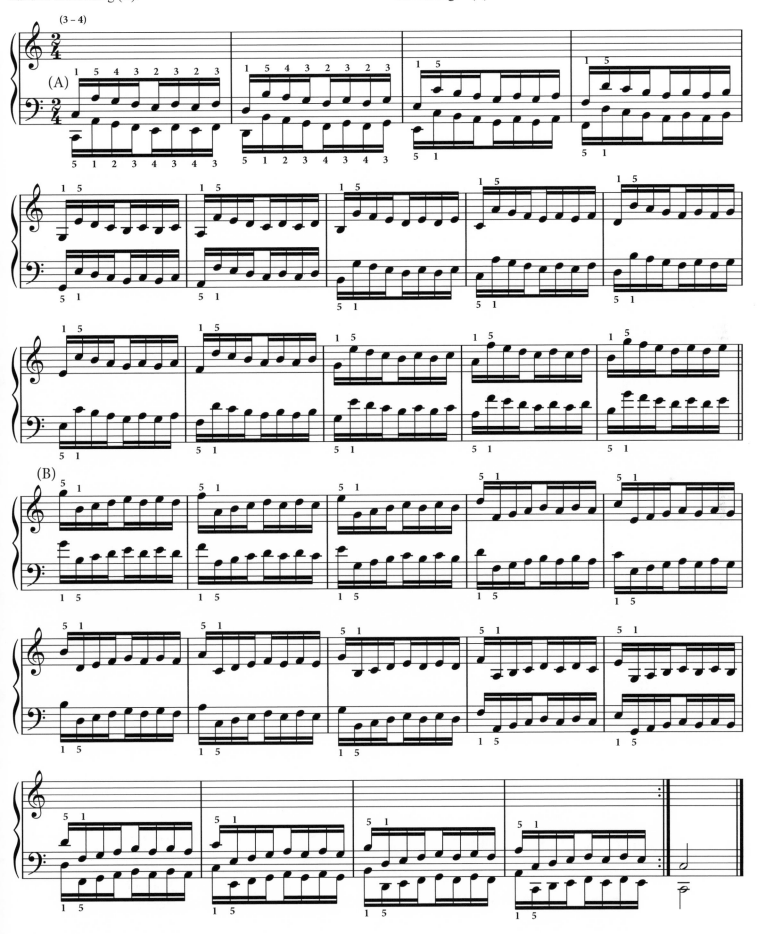

11

Another preparatory lesson for the trill with the 4th and 5th fingers of the right hand.

Weitere Vorübung zum Triller für den 4. und 5. Finger der rechten Hand.

12

Stretching between the 1st and 5th fingers, and training of the 3rd, 4th and 5th fingers.

Streckung zwischen dem 1. und 5. Finger und Training des 3., 4. und 5. Fingers.

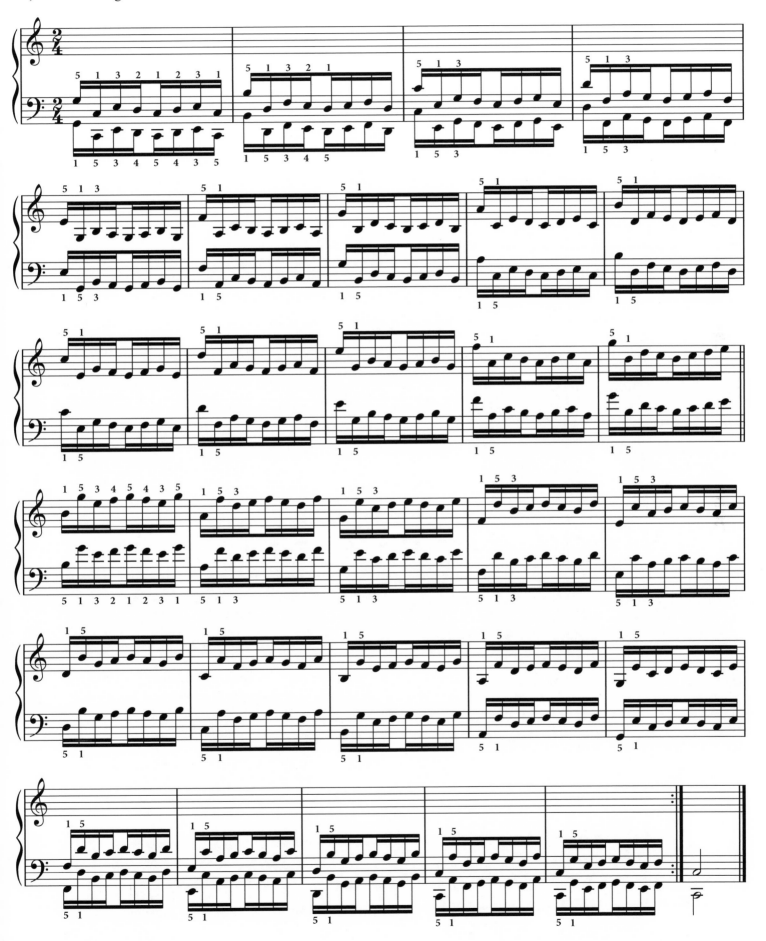

13

14

Another preparatory lesson for the trill with the 3rd and 4th fingers.

Vorübung zum Triller für den 3. und 4. Finger.

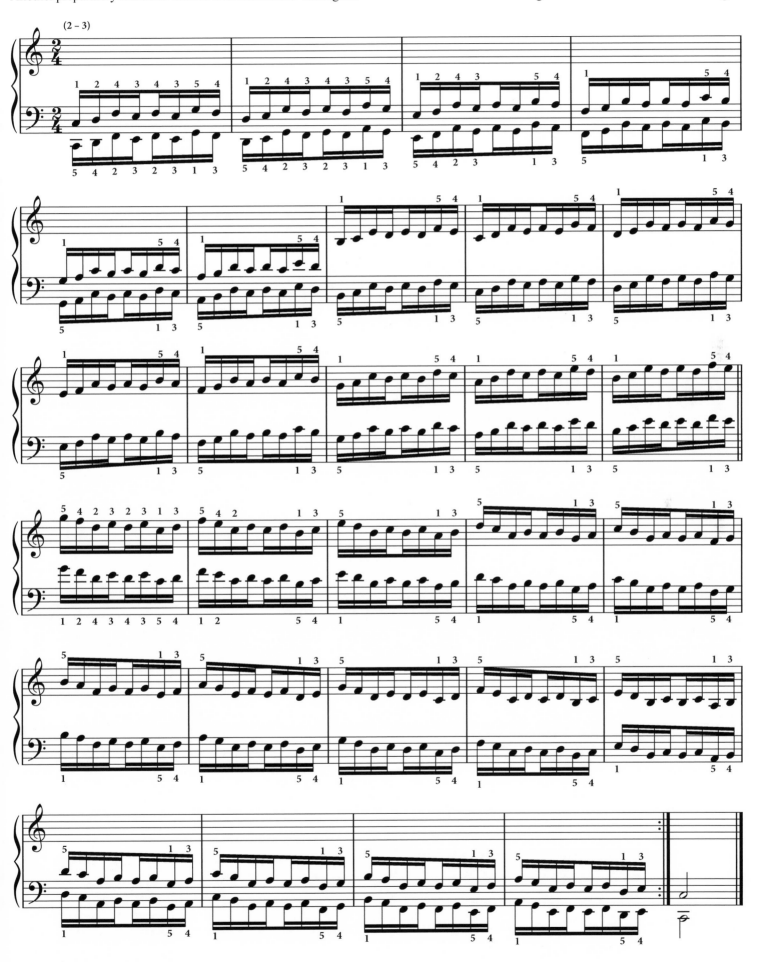

15

Stretching between the 1st and 2nd fingers and training of all five fingers.

Streckung zwischen dem 1. und 2. Finger und Training aller 5 Finger.

16

Stretching between the 3rd and 5th fingers, and training of the 3rd, 4th and 5th fingers.

Streckung zwischen dem 3. und 5. Finger und Training des 3., 4. und 5. Fingers.

17

Stretching between the 1st and 2nd, 2nd and 4th, 4th and 5th fingers, training of the 3rd, 4th and 5th fingers.

Streckung zwischen dem 1. und 2., 2. und 4., 4. und 5. Finger und Training des 3., 4. und 5. Fingers.

18

19

20

Stretching between the 2nd and 4th and 4th and 5th fingers, and training for the 2nd, 3rd and 4th fingers.

Streckung zwischen dem 2. und 4. und dem 4. und 5. Finger sowie Training des 2., 3. und 4. Fingers.

End of the First Part

As soon as the 1st part has been learnt, it should be played every day, once or twice, for some time, before beginning the study of the 2nd part, which is more difficult.

A real knowledge of this part will serve as a key to the difficulties which will be found in the 2nd part.

Ende des Ersten Teils

Wenn dieser Erste Teil eingehend erarbeitet wurde, sollte er eine Zeit lang täglich ein oder mehrere Male durchgespielt werden, bevor mit dem Zweiten, schwierigeren Teil begonnen wird.

Wer den Ersten Teil perfekt beherrscht, besitzt den Schlüssel für alle Schwierigkeiten des Zweiten Teils.

Second Part

A preparation to the transcendent exercises of the virtuose

Zweiter Teil

Schwierige Übungen, geeignet die Finger auf die virtuoseren Studien vorzubereiten

21

It should be noticed that the movement of the 3rd, 4th and 5th fingers of the left hand at the 1st beat of each bar (A) is reproduced in a contrary sense, by the same fingers of the right hand at the 2nd beat of the same bar (B).

Es ist zu beachten, dass die Bewegung des 3., 4. und 5. Fingers der linken Hand auf dem ersten Taktteil (A) in umgekehrter Richtung von denselben Fingern der rechten Hand auf dem zweiten Taktteil wiederholt wird (B).

The exercises of this Second Part, like those of the First, should be practised at the rate of 60 beats of the metronome, and the speed should be gradually increased to 108. All the following exercises, which are not marked, should be played thus. When there is any need to change this tempo, it will be written at the head of each exercise.

Die Etüden des Zweiten Teils wie die des Ersten zunächst im Zeitmaß 60 üben, um allmählich das Zeitmaß 108 zu erreichen. In dieser Weise sind alle folgenden Übungen zu erarbeiten, auch wenn kein Zeitmaß angegeben ist. Sollte für eine dieser Übungen ein anderes Tempo gelten, so wird dies jeweils über dem ersten Notensystem angezeigt.

22

All the exercises of this Second Part should be studied as is indicated in the First Part at the head of page 10; therefore while studying these exercises, stops should be made only at the last notes of the pages 31, 33, 35, 37, 39, 41, 43, and 45.

Die Übungen dieses Zweiten Teils sind in derselben Weise zu studieren wie es für den Ersten Teil auf S. 10 empfohlen wurde. Es wird also nur auf den letzten Noten der Seiten 31, 33, 35, 37, 39, 41, 43 und 45 innegehalten.

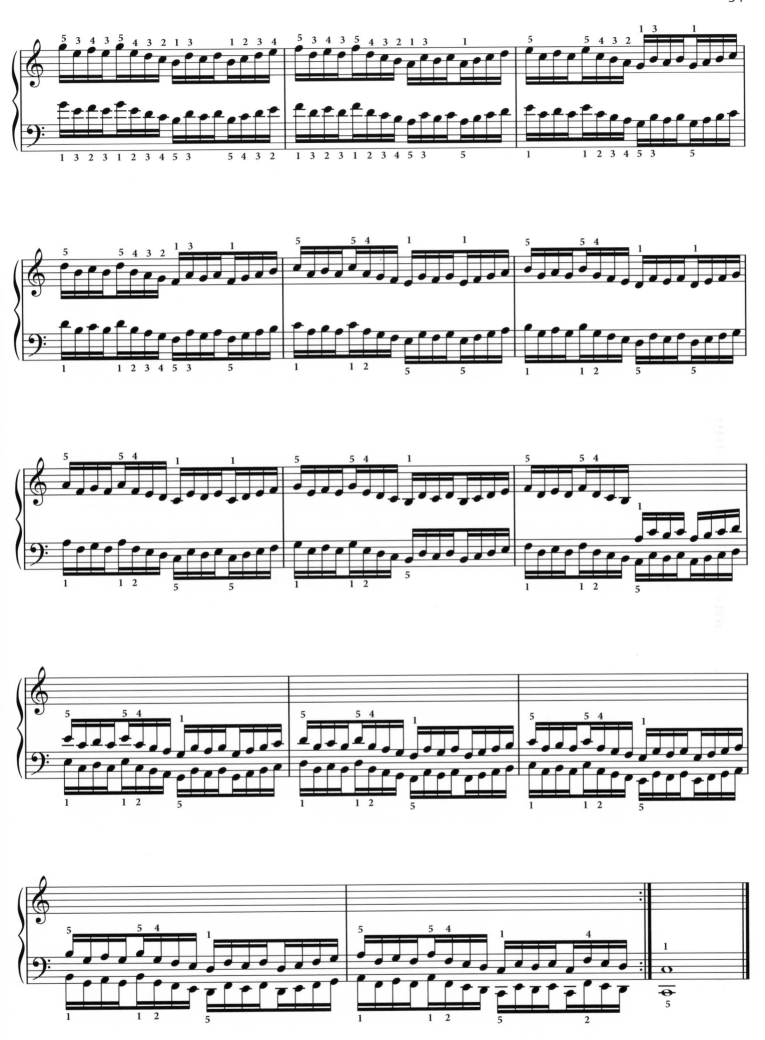

23

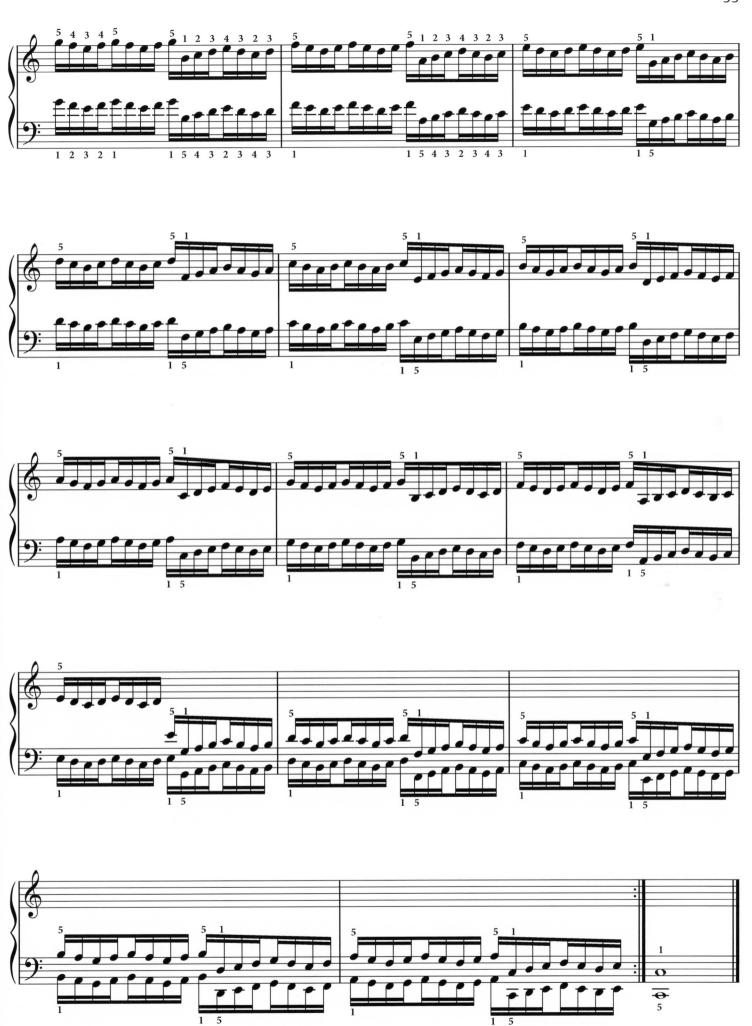

24

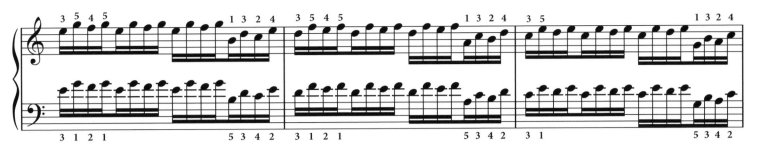

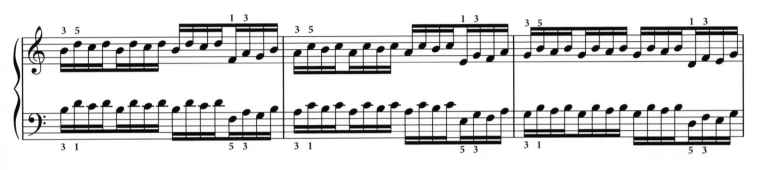

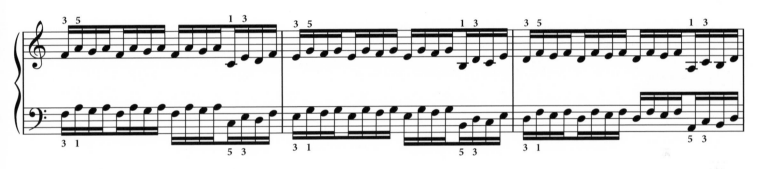

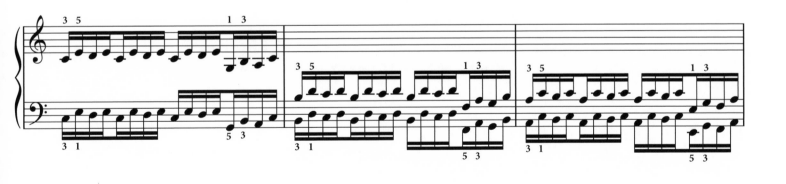

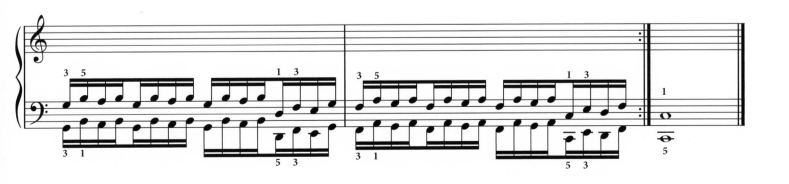

25

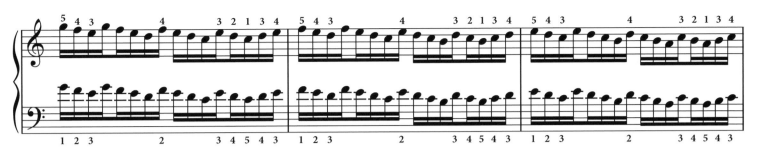

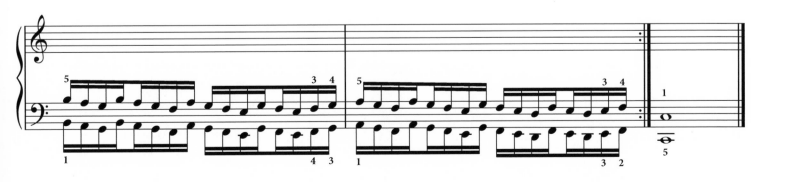

26

40

27

Preparatory exercise for the trill with the 4th and 5th fingers.

Trillervorübung für den 4. und 5. Finger.

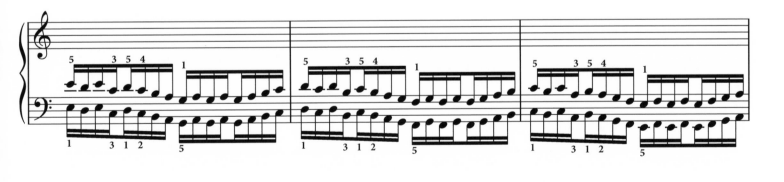

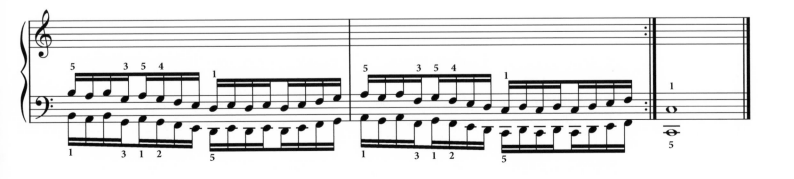

28

29

Preparatory exercise for the trill with all 5 fingers.

Trillervorübung für alle 5 Finger.

© 2016 Schott Music GmbH & Co. KG, Mainz

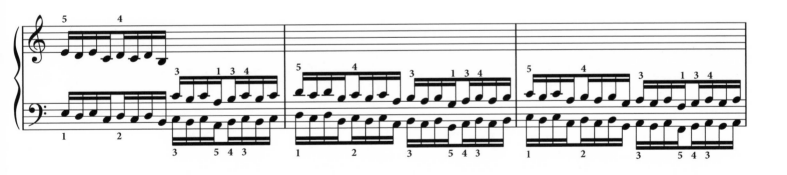

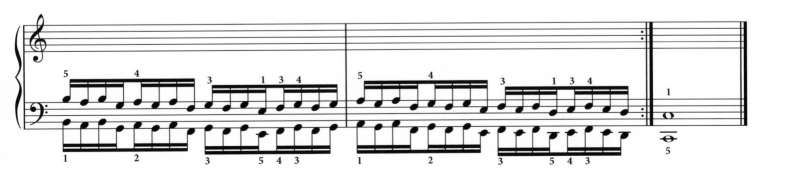

30

Trill alternately with 1st and 2nd and with 4th and 5th fingers.

In dieser Übung ist der Triller abwechselnd mit dem 1. und 2. und dem 4. und 5. Finger auszuführen.

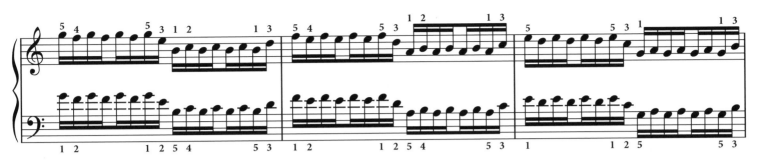

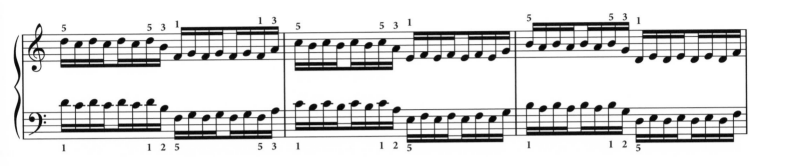

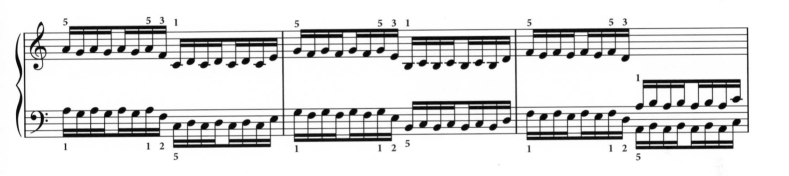

31

Exercises for stretching all 5 fingers.

(1 – 2 – 3 – 4 – 5)

32

Passing the thumb under the 2nd finger.

Untersetzen des Daumens unter den 2. Finger.

♩. = 40–72

Repeat this bar 4 times
Diesen Takt 4-mal wiederholen

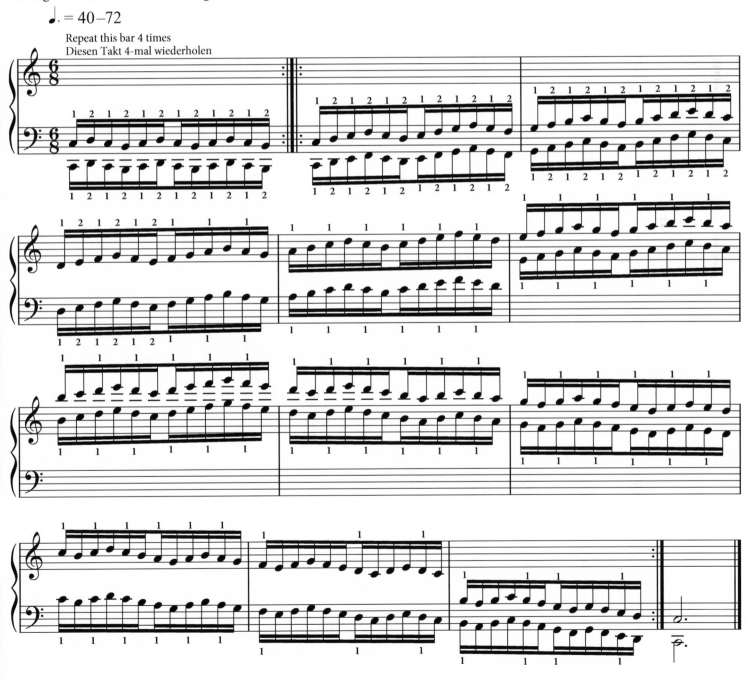

33

Passing the thumb under the 3rd finger.

Untersetzen des Daumens unter den 3. Finger.

♩. = 40–72

Repeat this bar 4 times
Diesen Takt 4-mal wiederholen

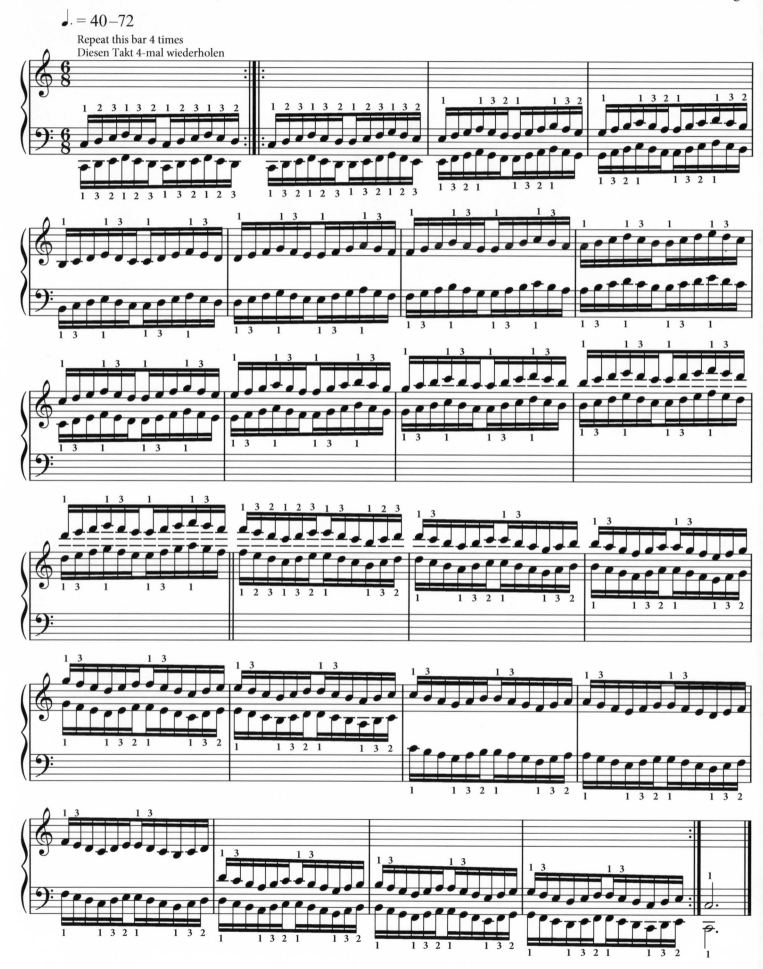

34

Passing the thumb under the 4th finger.

♩ = 60–108

Repeat this bar 10 times
Diesen Takt 10-mal wiederholen

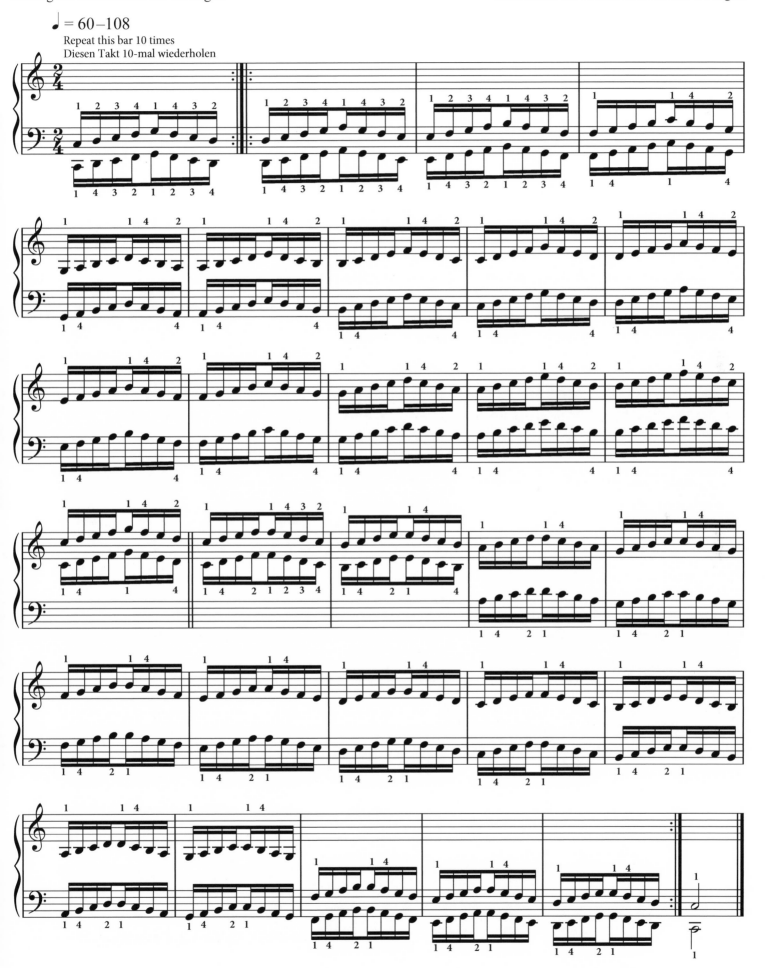

35

Passing the thumb under the 5th finger; this exercise is of the greatest importance.

Untersetzen des Daumens unter den 5. Finger. Diese Übung ist von höchster Wichtigkeit.

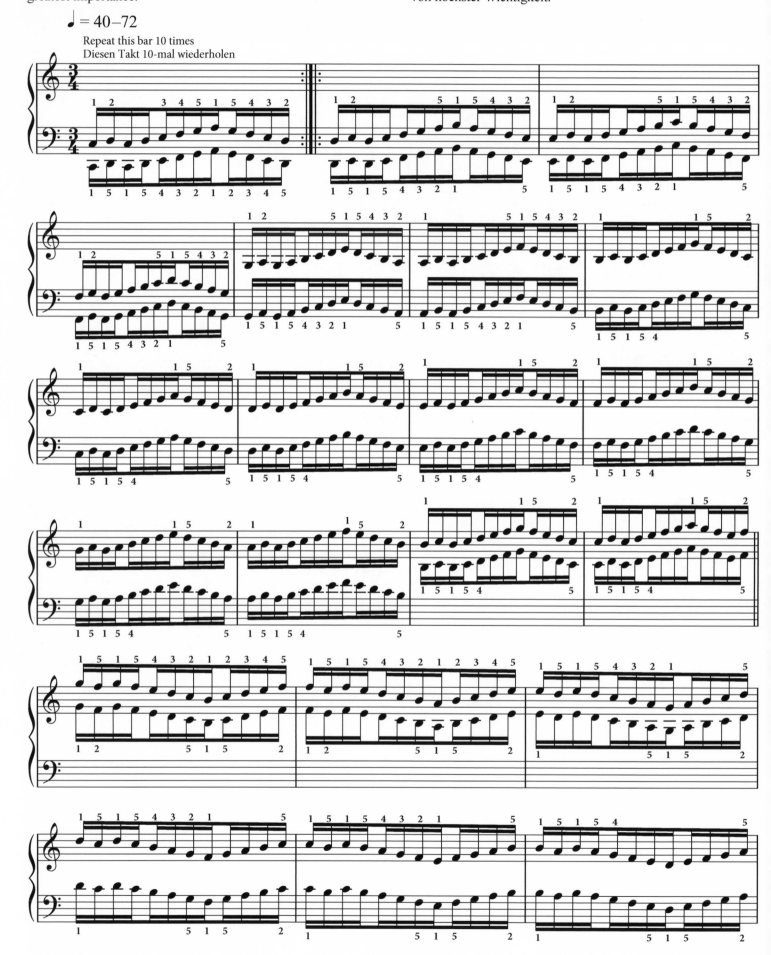

36

Another example for passing the thumb under.

Ein anderes Beispiel für das Untersetzen des Daumens.

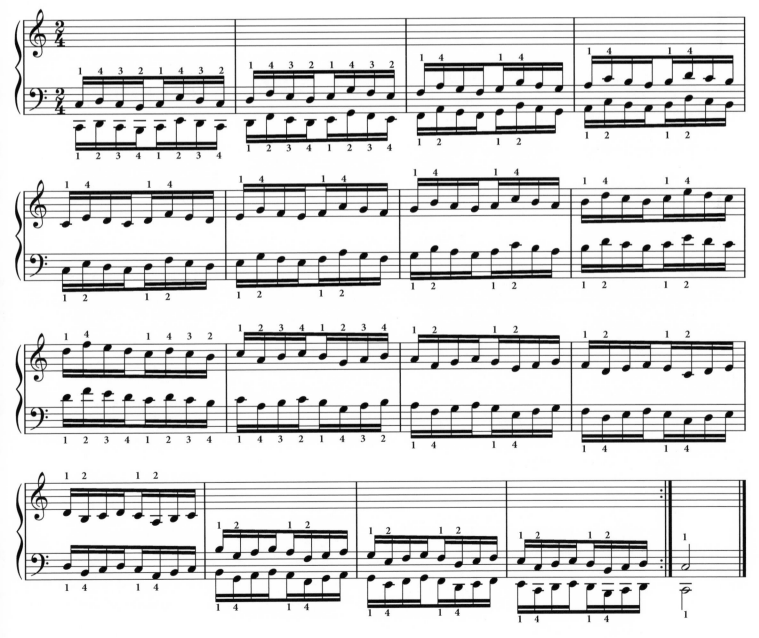

37

Special exercise for passing the thumb under. The whole of this line to be played with the thumbs only.

Sonderübung für das Untersetzen des Daumens. Die ganze Parallelbewegung wird nur von den Daumen ausgeführt.

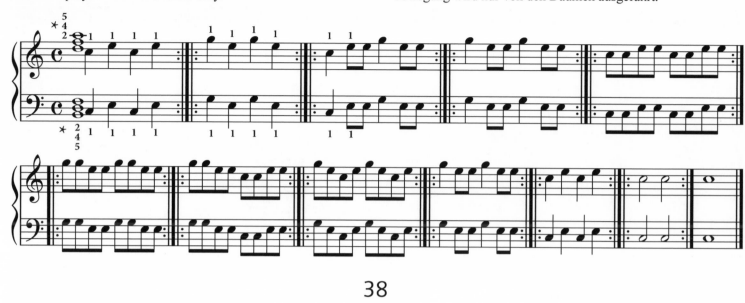

38

Preparatory exercise for the study of scales.

Vorübung für das Tonleiterspiel.

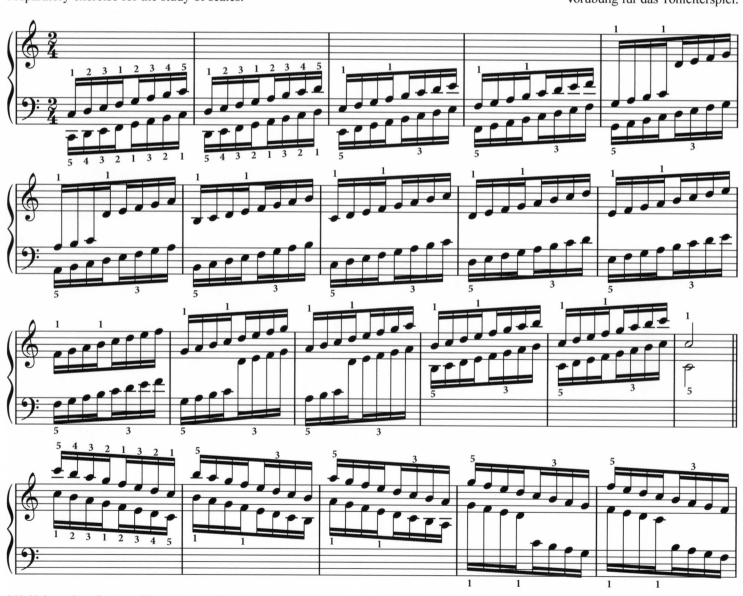

* Hold down these 3 notes with each hand while playing these 12 bars.

* Die Tasten der beiden Akkorde tonlos niedergedrückt halten, während alle 12 Takte gespielt werden.

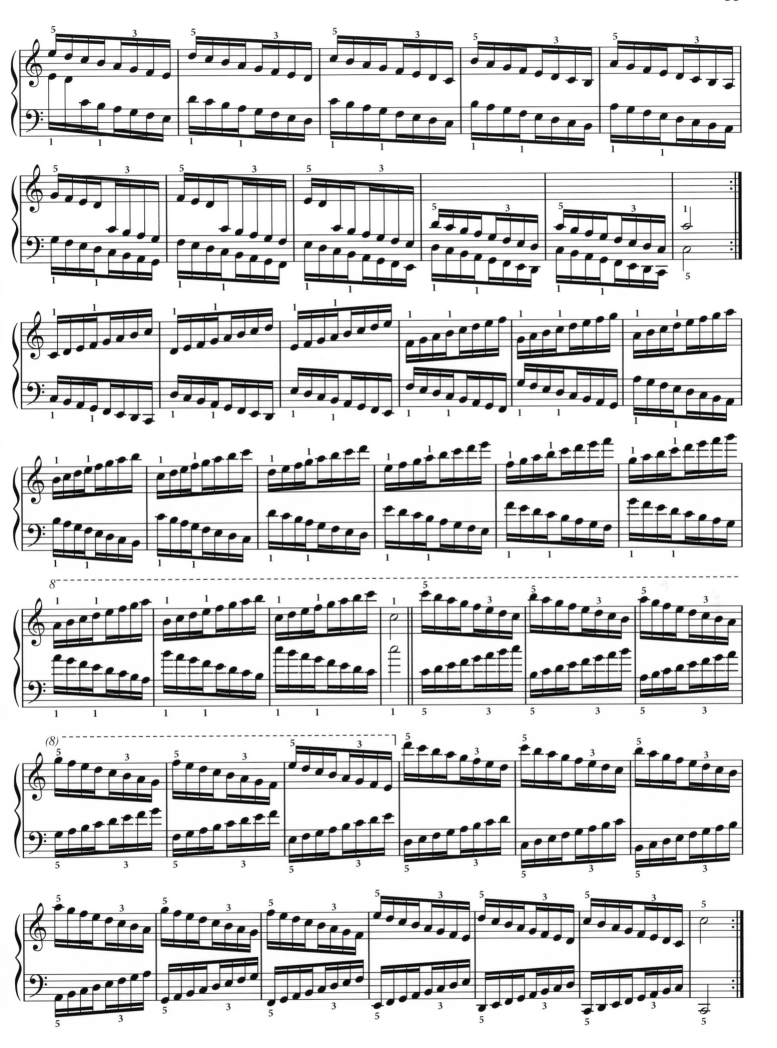

39

Major scales in octaves * Durtonleitern in Oktaven *

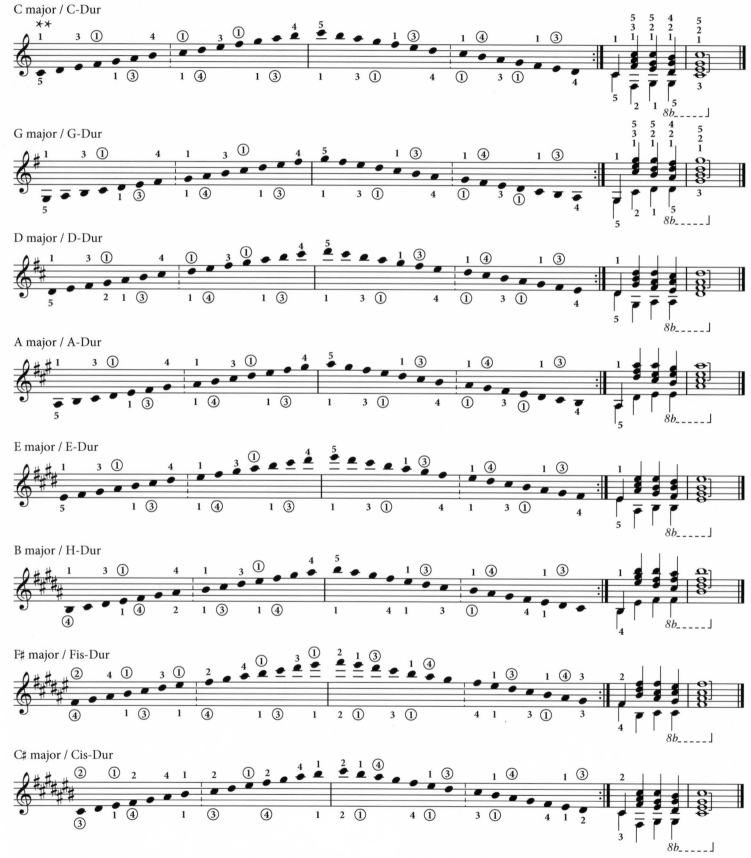

C major / C-Dur

G major / G-Dur

D major / D-Dur

A major / A-Dur

E major / E-Dur

B major / H-Dur

F♯ major / Fis-Dur

C♯ major / Cis-Dur

* All these scales are to be practised over a range of 2, 3 and 4 octaves, with varied rhythm.

** The fingering for the right hand is indicated above the notes, the left hand fingering below them. The figures in circles indicate an exceptional fingering. This also applies to the following exercises.

* Alle Tonleitern sind mit wechselndem Rhythmus über 2, 3 und 4 Oktaven zu üben.

** Der Fingersatz für die rechte Hand steht über, der für die linke Hand unter den Noten. Die eingekreisten Zahlen bedeuten einen besonderen Fingersatz. Dies gilt auch für die nachfolgenden Übungen.

F major / F-Dur

B♭ major / B-Dur

E♭ major / Es-Dur

A♭ major / As-Dur

D♭ major / Des-Dur

G♭ major / Ges-Dur

C♭ major / Ces-Dur

Chromatic scale   Chromatische Tonleiter

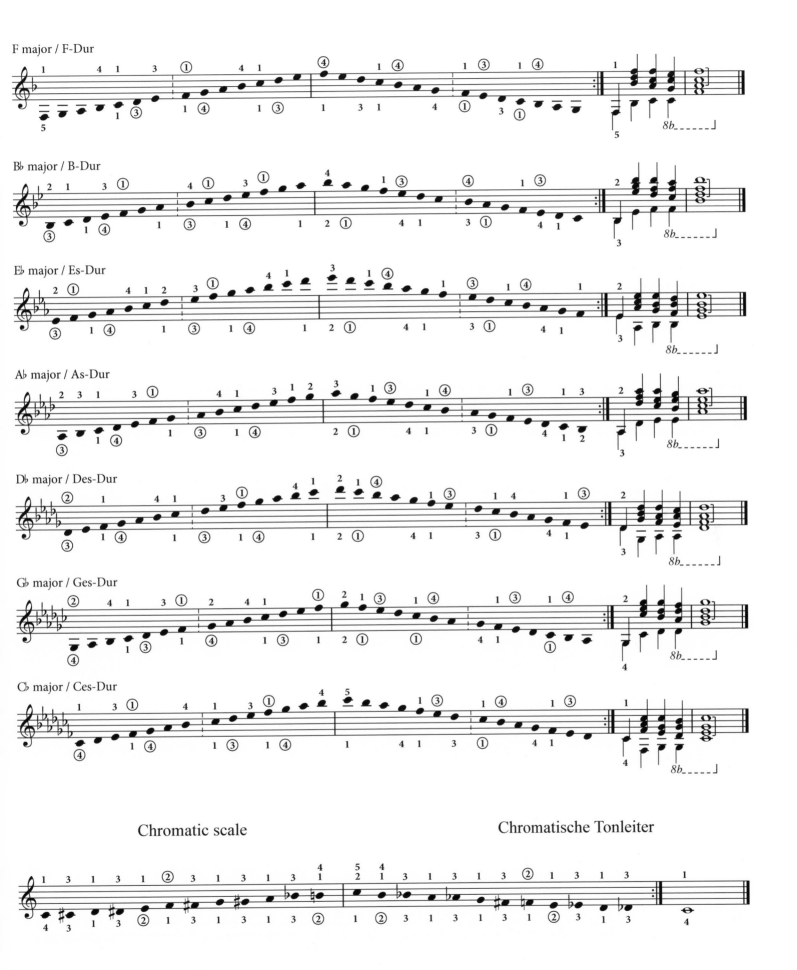

Broken major triads (arpeggios) *

Gebrochene Durdreiklänge (Arpeggien) *

Root position / Grundstellung   1st Inversion / 1. Umkehrung   2nd Inversion / 2. Umkehrung

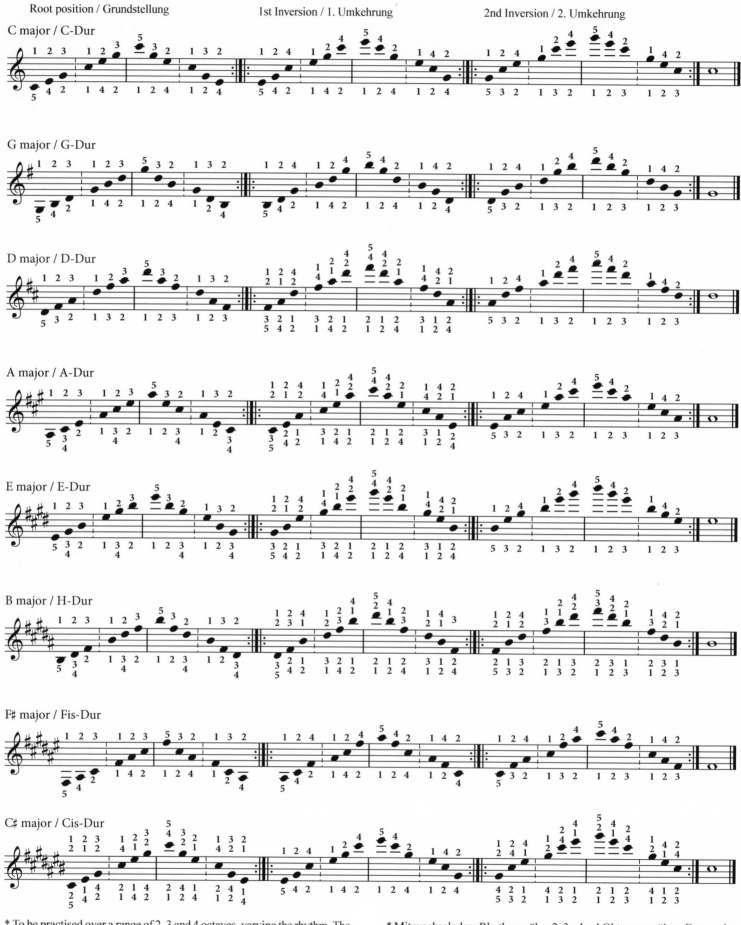

* To be practised over a range of 2, 3 and 4 octaves, varying the rhythm. The second fingering written above the first for the right hand, and below for the left hand, is used by some composers, who apply the fingering for the scale of C to all, or almost all, the scales.

* Mit wechselndem Rhythmus über 2, 3 oder 4 Oktaven zu üben. Der zweite Fingersatz (der für die rechte Hand über dem ersten, für die linke Hand darunter steht) wird von einigen Komponisten empfohlen, die den Fingersatz der C-Durtonleiter für alle oder fast alle Tonleitern vorschreiben.

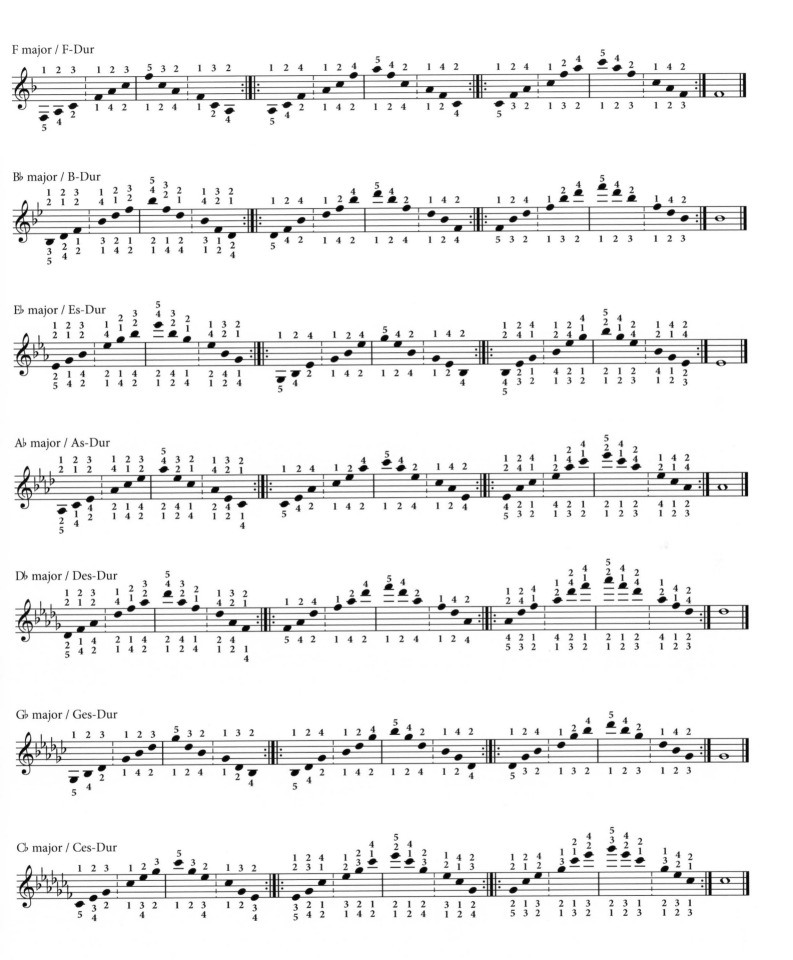

Minor scales in octaves

A minor / a-Moll

E minor / e-Moll

B minor / h-Moll

F# minor / fis-Moll

C# minor / cis-Moll

G# minor / gis-Moll

D# minor / dis-Moll

A# minor / ais-Moll

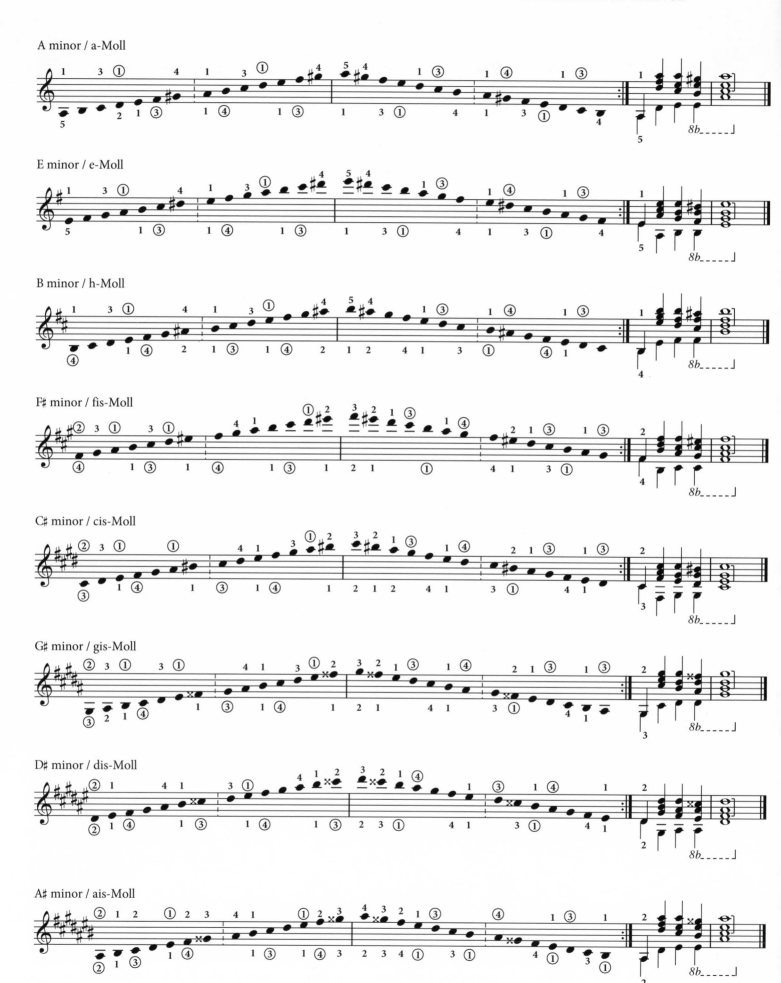

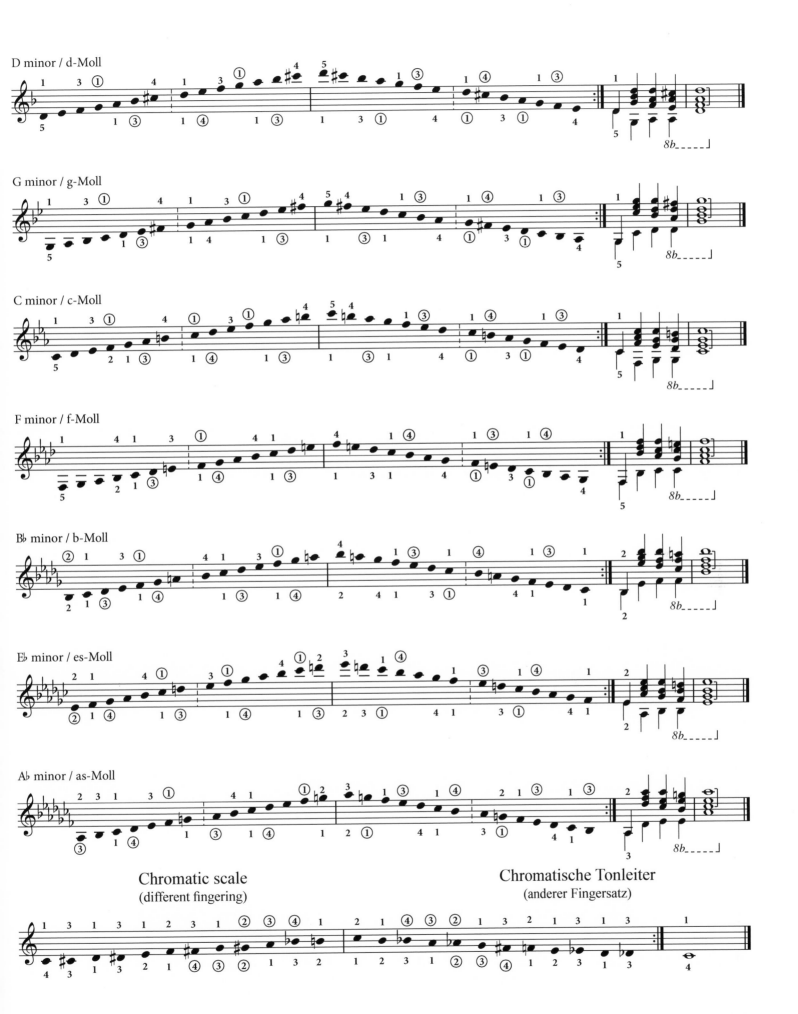

D minor / d-Moll

G minor / g-Moll

C minor / c-Moll

F minor / f-Moll

B♭ minor / b-Moll

E♭ minor / es-Moll

A♭ minor / as-Moll

Chromatic scale
(different fingering)

Chromatische Tonleiter
(anderer Fingersatz)

Broken minor triads (arpeggios)

Gebrochene Molldreiklänge (Arpeggien)

Root position / Grundstellung   1st Inversion / 1. Umkehrung   2nd Inversion / 2. Umkehrung

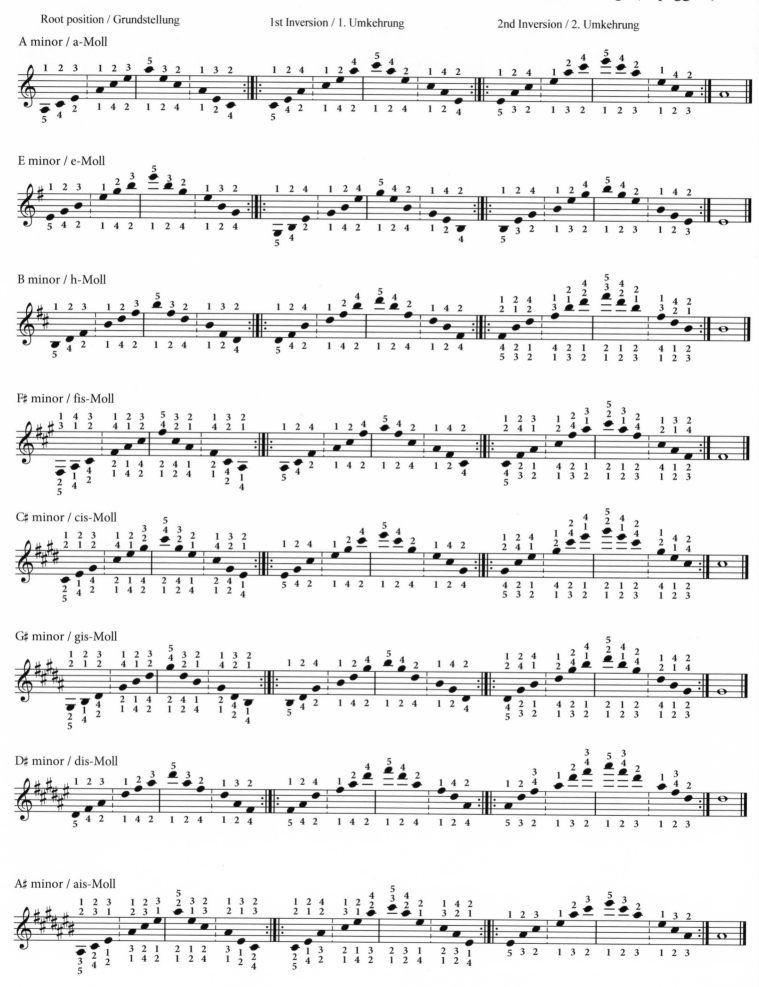

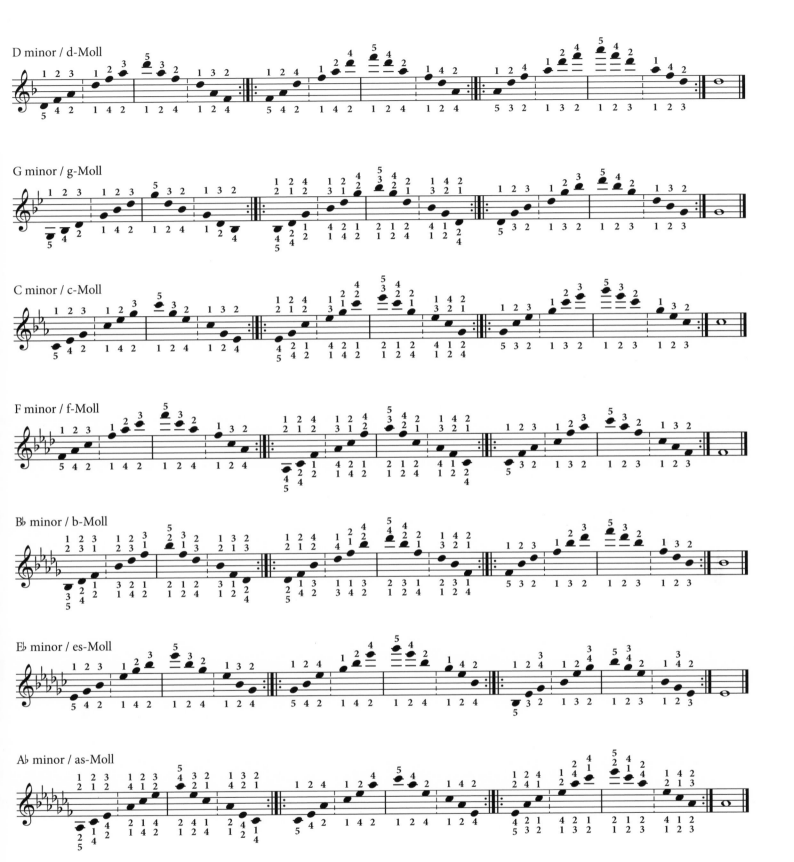

40

Major scales in contrary motion, commencing in unison

Durtonleitern in Gegenbewegung mit dem Einklang anfangend

Minor scales (related to the adjacent major scales) in contrary motion, commencing in unison

Molltonleitern den nebenstehenden Durtonleitern verwandt, in Gegenbewegung, mit dem Einklang anfangend

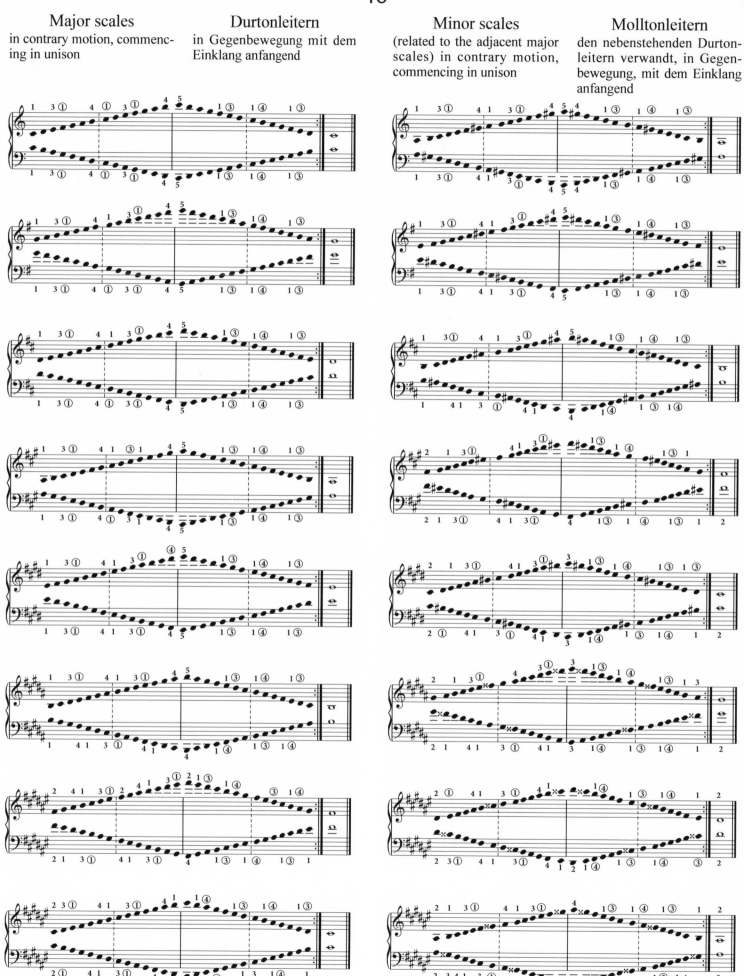

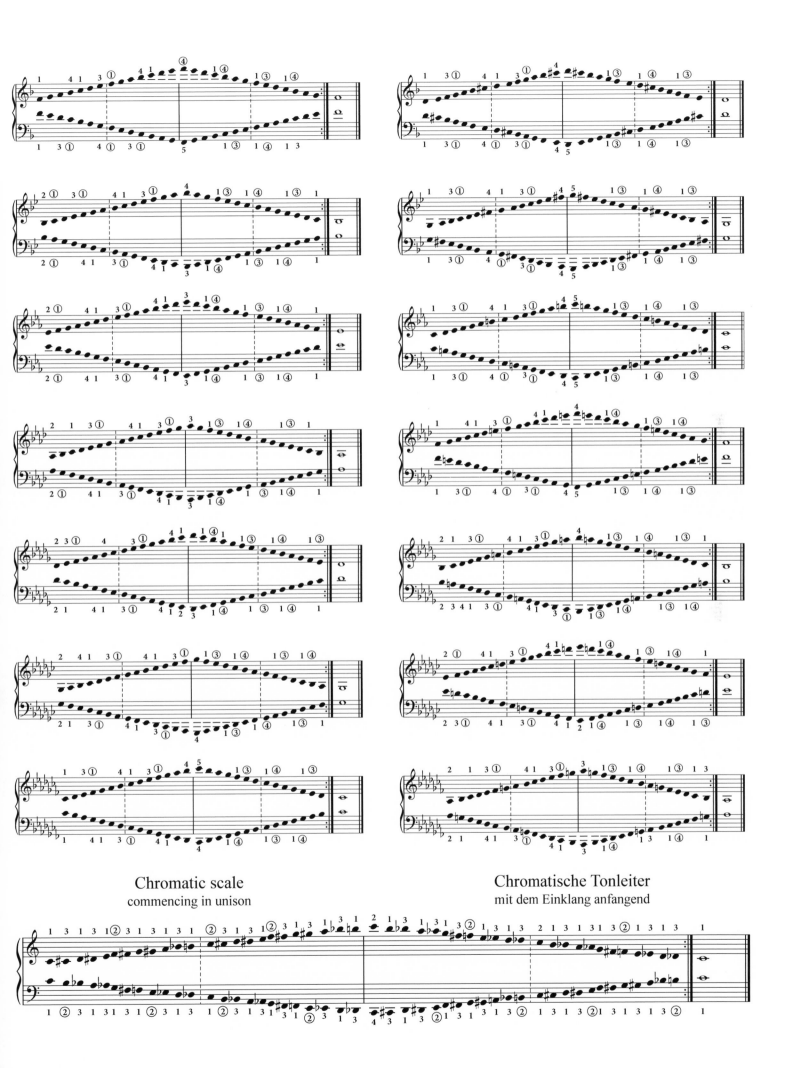

Chromatic scale
commencing in unison

Chromatische Tonleiter
mit dem Einklang anfangend

Broken major triads
in contrary motion, commencing on the tonic

Gebrochene Durdreiklänge
in Gegenbewegung, mit der Tonika beginnend

Root position / Grundstellung · 1st Inversion / 1. Umkehrung · 2nd Inversion / 2. Umkehrung

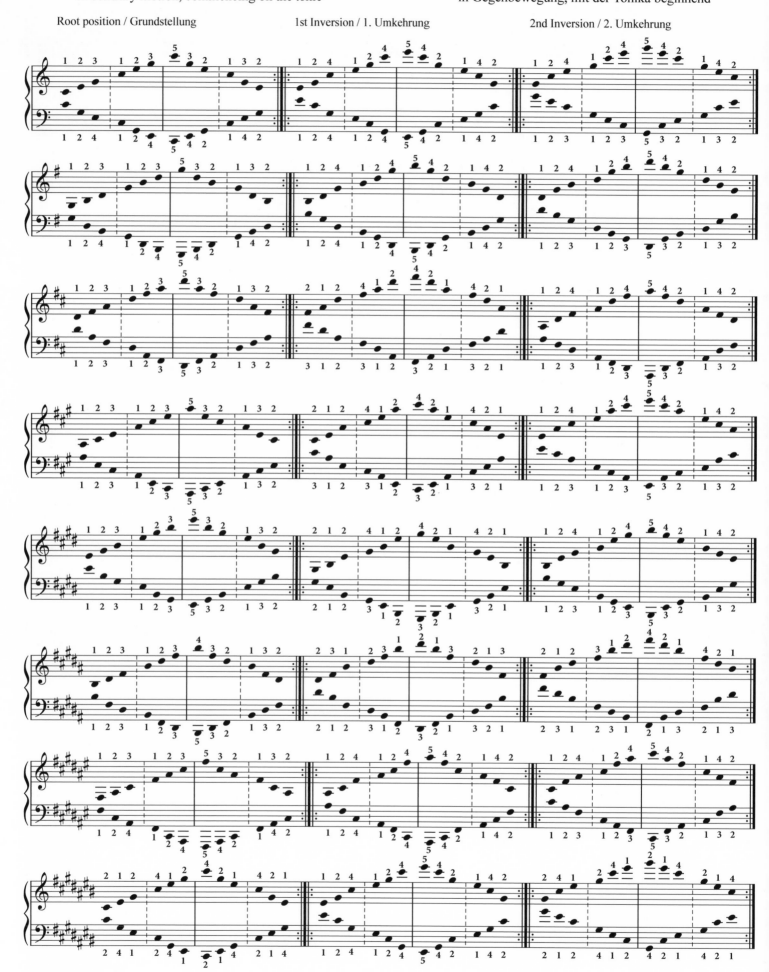

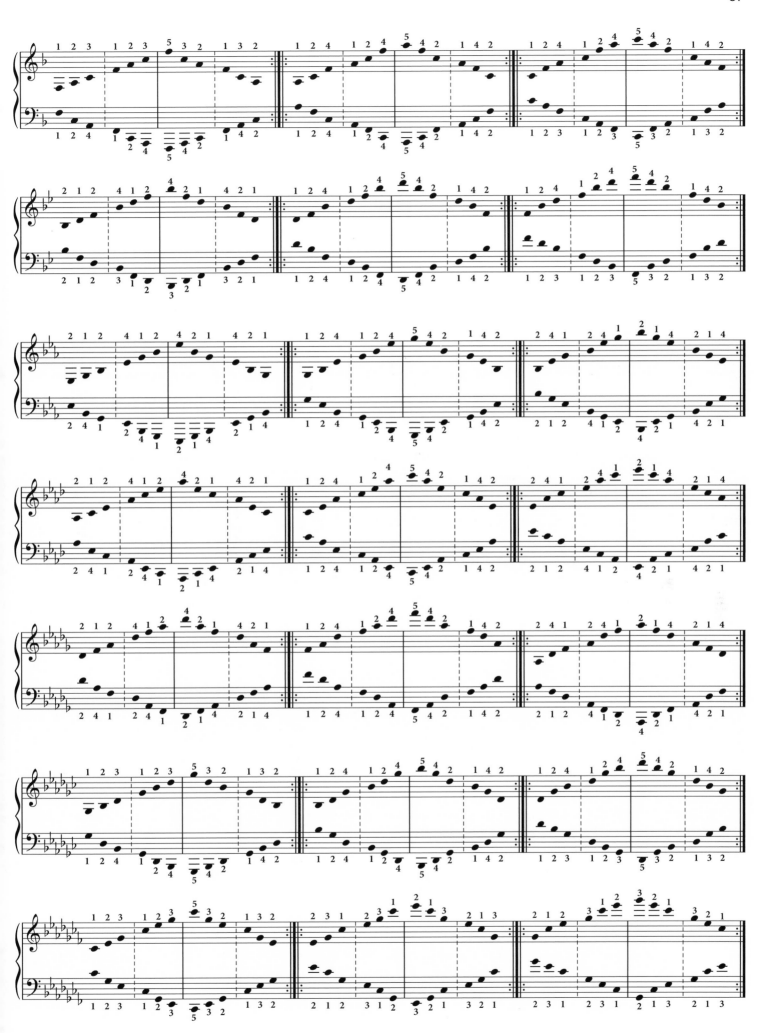

Broken minor triads
in contrary motion, commencing on the tonic

Gebrochene Molldreiklänge
in Gegenbewegung, mit der Tonika beginnend

Root position / Grundstellung   1st Inversion / 1. Umkehrung   2nd Inversion / 2. Umkehrung

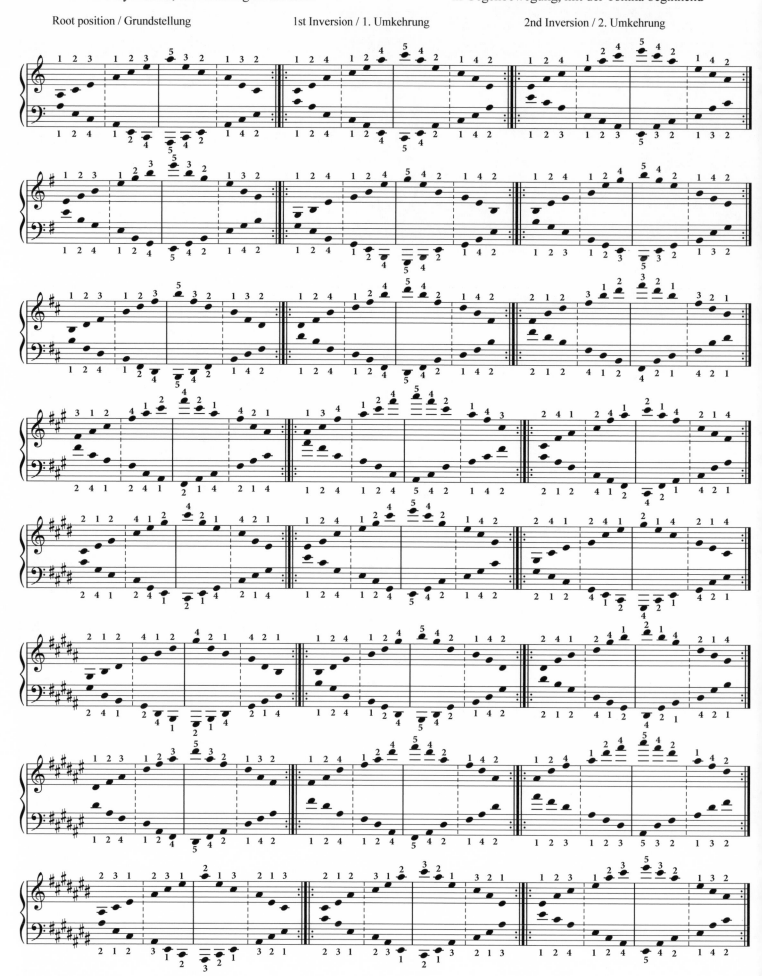

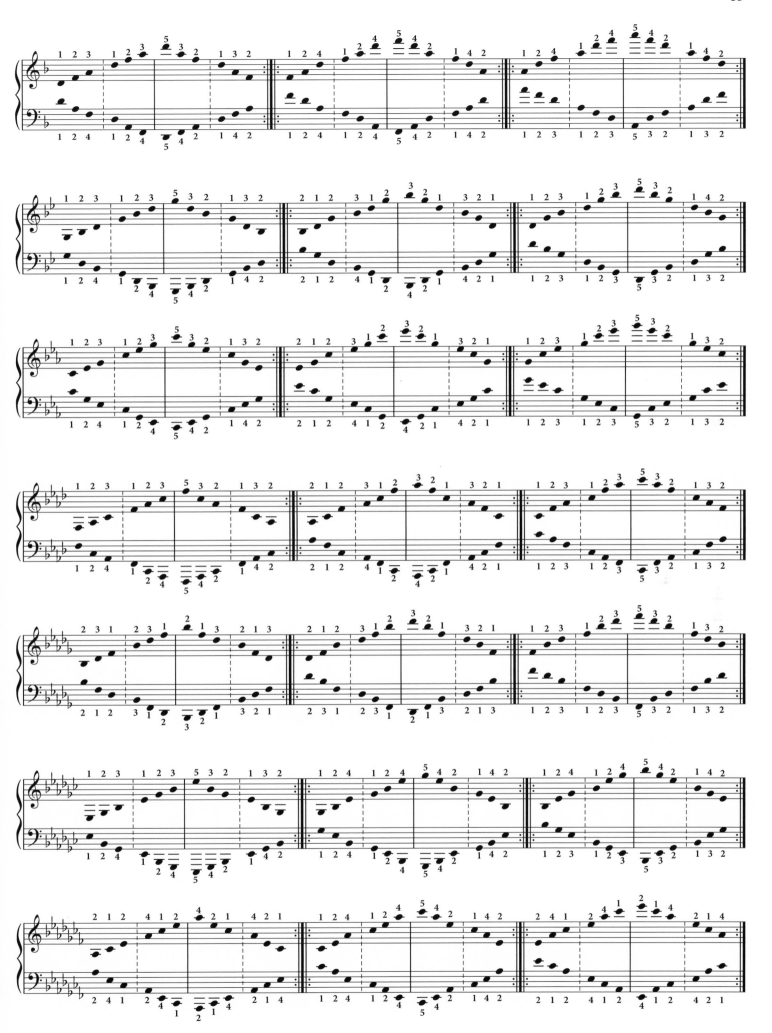

41

Major scales in thirds * Durtonleitern in Terzen *

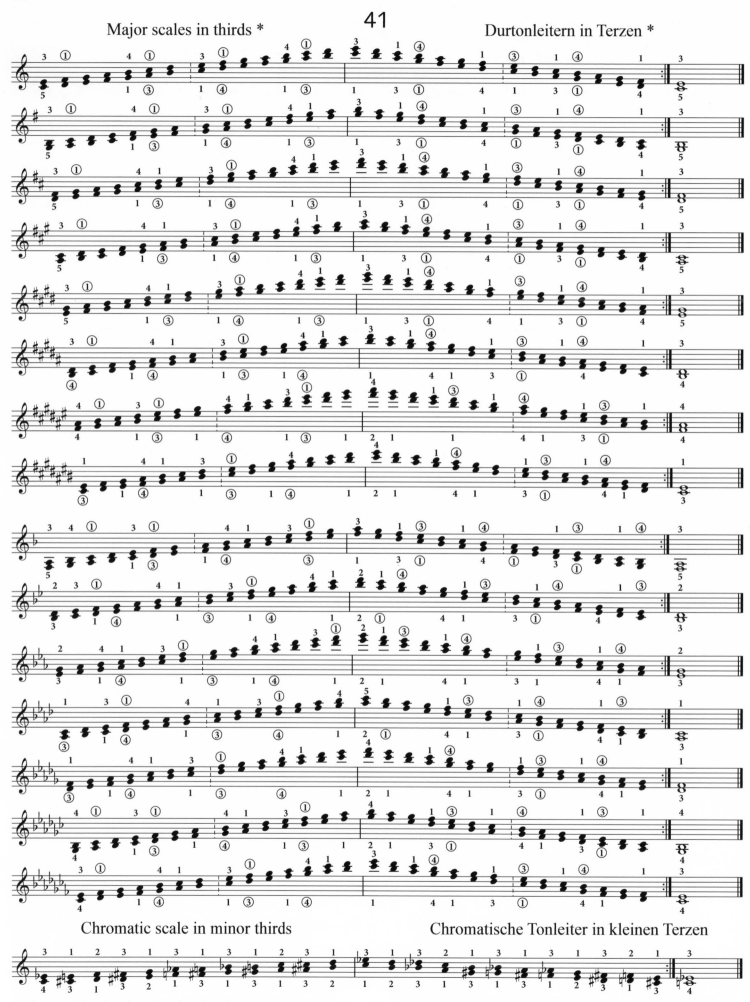

Chromatic scale in minor thirds Chromatische Tonleiter in kleinen Terzen

* When practising them in tenths, place the left hand an octave lower.

* Beim Spielen in Dezimen wird die linke Hand eine Oktave tiefer angeschlagen.

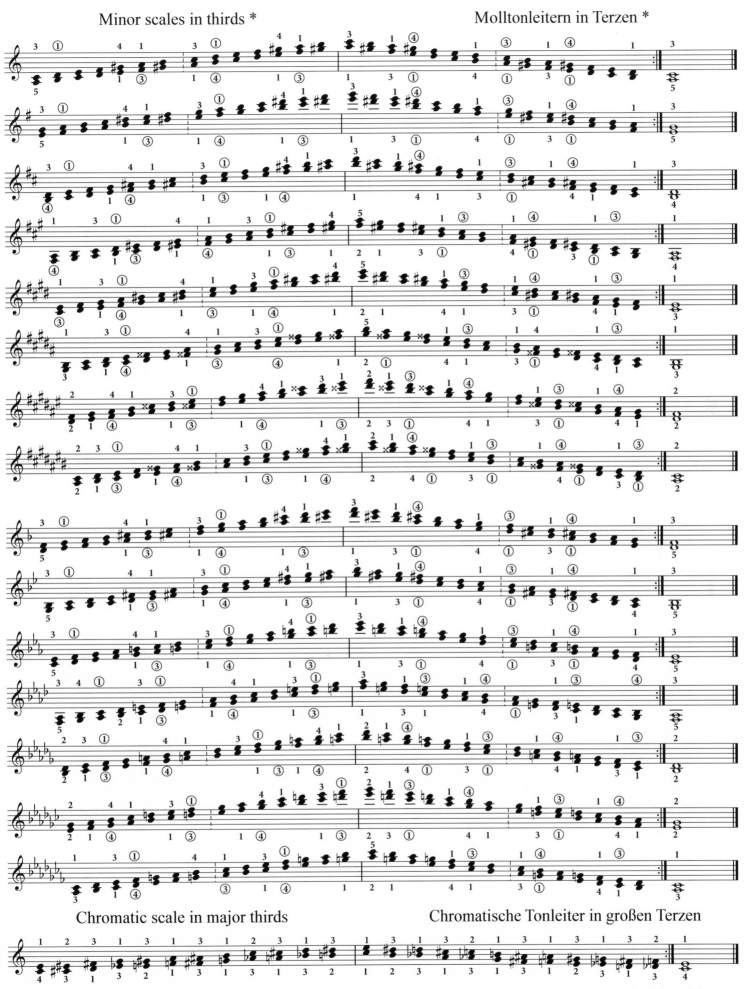

Minor scales in thirds *

Molltonleitern in Terzen *

Chromatic scale in major thirds

Chromatische Tonleiter in großen Terzen

* When practising them in tenths, place the left hand an octave lower.

* Beim Spielen in Dezimen wird die linke Hand eine Oktave tiefer angeschlagen.

Broken major triads

(arpeggios); the left hand commences with the tonic, the right hand with the third above.

Gebrochene Durdreiklänge

(Arpeggien); die linke Hand beginnt mit der Tonika, die rechte Hand mit der Terz darüber.

Root position / Grundstellung   1st Inversion / 1. Umkehrung   2nd Inversion / 2. Umkehrung

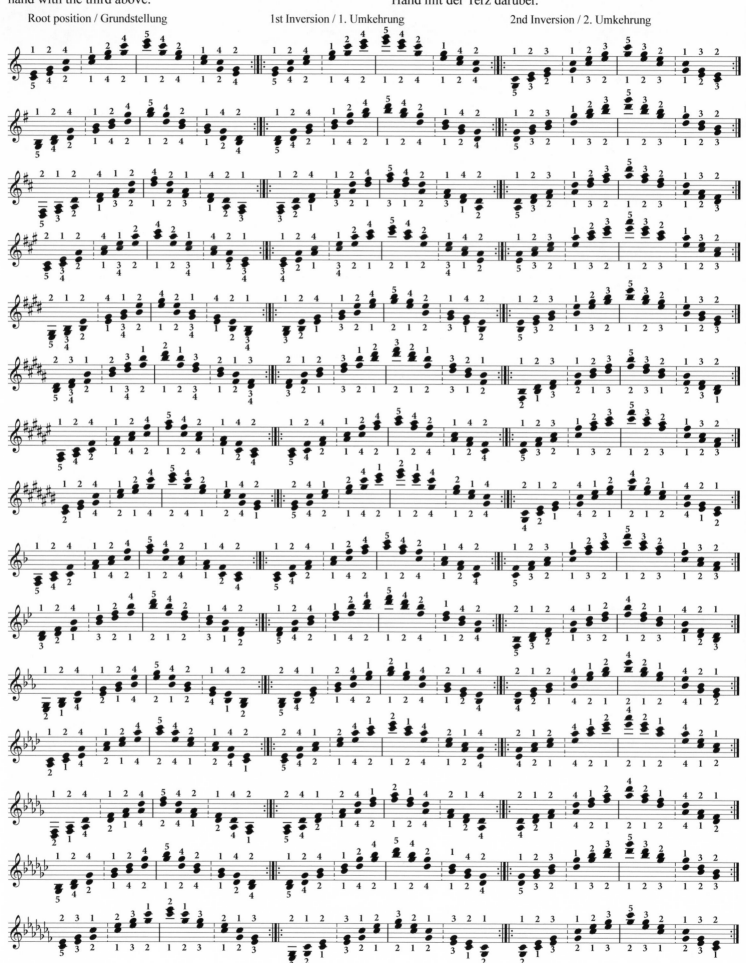

Broken minor triads

(related to the adjacent major triads); the left hand commences
with the tonic, the right hand with the third above.

Gebrochene Molldreiklänge

den nebenstehenden Durdreiklängen verwandt; die linke Hand
beginnt mit der Tonika, die rechte Hand mit der Terz darüber.

Root position / Grundstellung   1st Inversion / 1. Umkehrung   2nd Inversion / 2. Umkehrung

© 2016 Schott Music GmbH & Co. KG, Mainz

74

Major scales in sixths

Durtonleitern in Sexten

Chromatic scale in major sixths

Chromatische Tonleiter in großen Sexten

Minor scales in sixths

Molltonleitern in Sexten

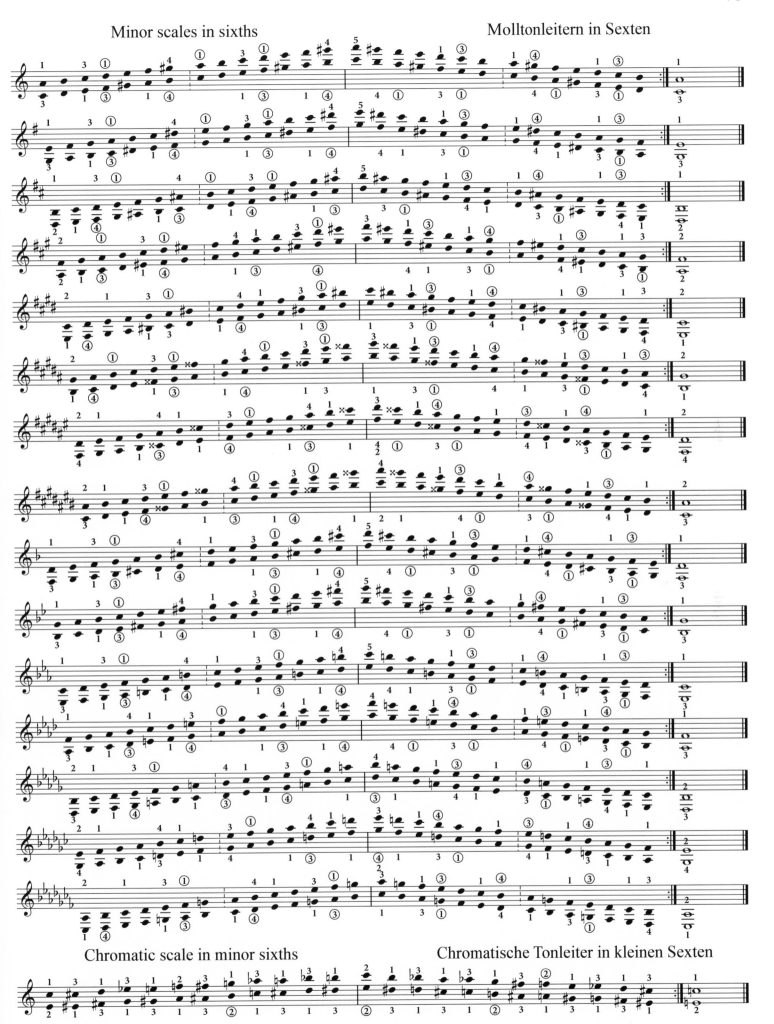

Chromatic scale in minor sixths

Chromatische Tonleiter in kleinen Sexten

Broken major triads

The right hand commences with the tonic, the left hand on the third (mediant).

Gebrochene Durdreiklänge

Die rechte Hand fängt mit der Tonika an, die linke Hand mit der Terz (Mediante).

Root position / Grundstellung   1st Inversion / 1. Umkehrung   2nd Inversion / 2. Umkehrung

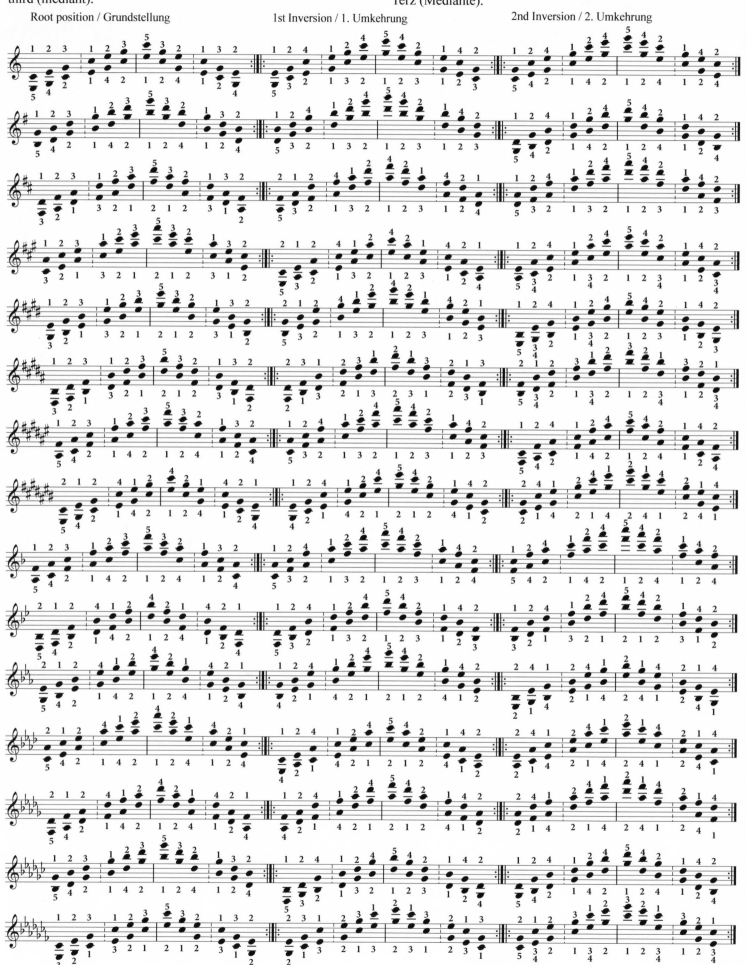

Broken minor triads

(related minor to the adjacent major triads), the right hand commences with the tonic, the left hand on the third (mediant).

Gebrochene Molldreiklänge

den nebenstehenden Durdreiklängen verwandt; die rechte Hand fängt mit der Tonika an, die linke Hand mit der Terz (Mediante).

Root position / Grundstellung — 1st Inversion / 1. Umkehrung — 2nd Inversion / 2. Umkehrung

42

Broken chords of the dominant seventh
with the octave

Gebrochene Dominant-Septakkorde
in Oktaven

Root position / Grundstellung 1st Inversion / 1. Umkehrung 2nd Inversion / 2. Umkehrung 3rd Inversion / 3. Umkehrung

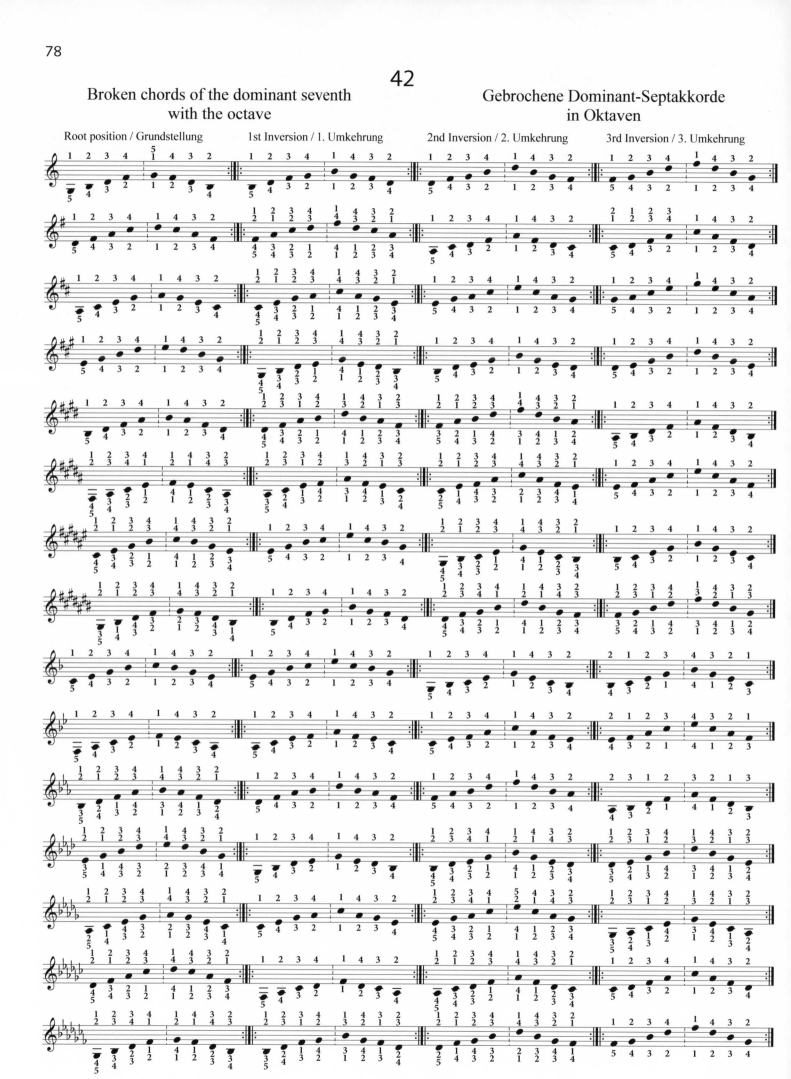

Broken chords of the dominant seventh

The left hand commences with the dominant, the right hand with the tenth above. *

Gebrochene Dominant-Septakkorde

Die linke Hand fängt mit der Dominante an, die rechte Hand mit der oberen Dezime. *

Root position / Grundstellung   1st Inversion / 1. Umkehrung   2nd Inversion / 2. Umkehrung   3rd Inversion / 3. Umkehrung

* When executing these arpeggios the left hand commencing on the tonic, the right hand on the third above, imagine the upper part an octave lower.

* Wenn bei der Ausführung dieser Arpeggien die linke Hand mit der Tonika anfängt, die rechte Hand mit der oberen Terz, denke man sich die obere Stimme eine Oktave tiefer geschrieben.

Broken chords of the dominant seventh

The left hand begins with the dominant, the right hand with the fifth above.

Gebrochene Dominant-Septakkorde

Die linke Hand beginnt mit der Dominante, die rechte Hand mit der Quinte darüber.

Root position / Grundstellung   1st Inversion / 1. Umkehrung   2nd Inversion / 2. Umkehrung   3rd Inversion / 3. Umkehrung

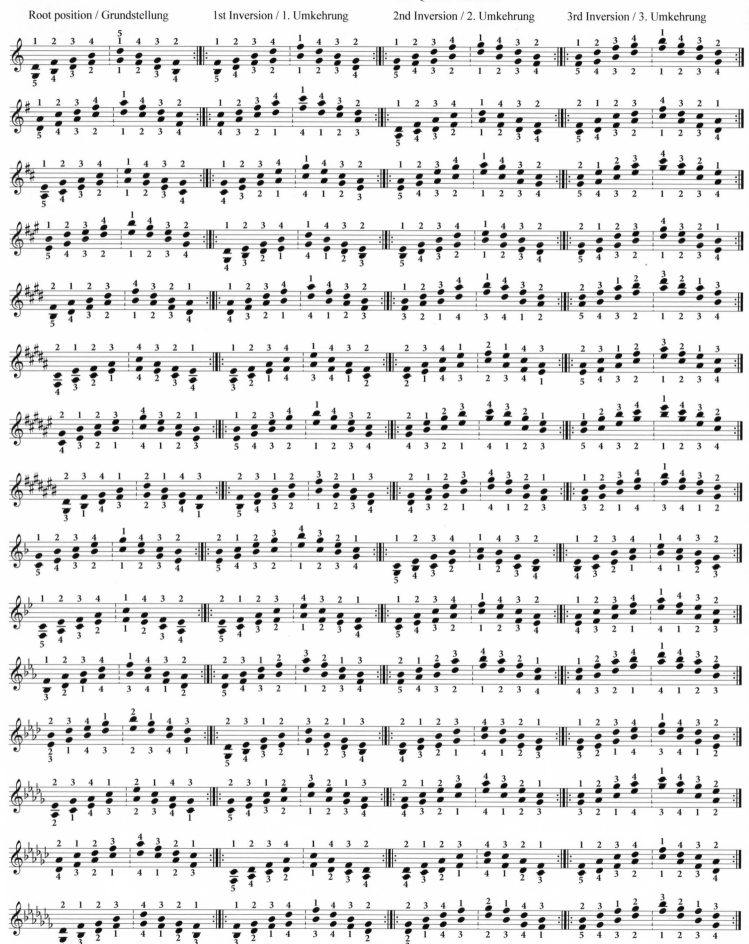

Broken chords of the dominant seventh

The left hand begins with the dominant, the right hand with its seventh.

Gebrochene Dominant-Septakkorde

Die linke Hand beginnt mit der Dominante, die rechte Hand mit deren Septime.

Root position / Grundstellung   1st Inversion / 1. Umkehrung   2nd Inversion / 2. Umkehrung   3rd Inversion / 3. Umkehrung

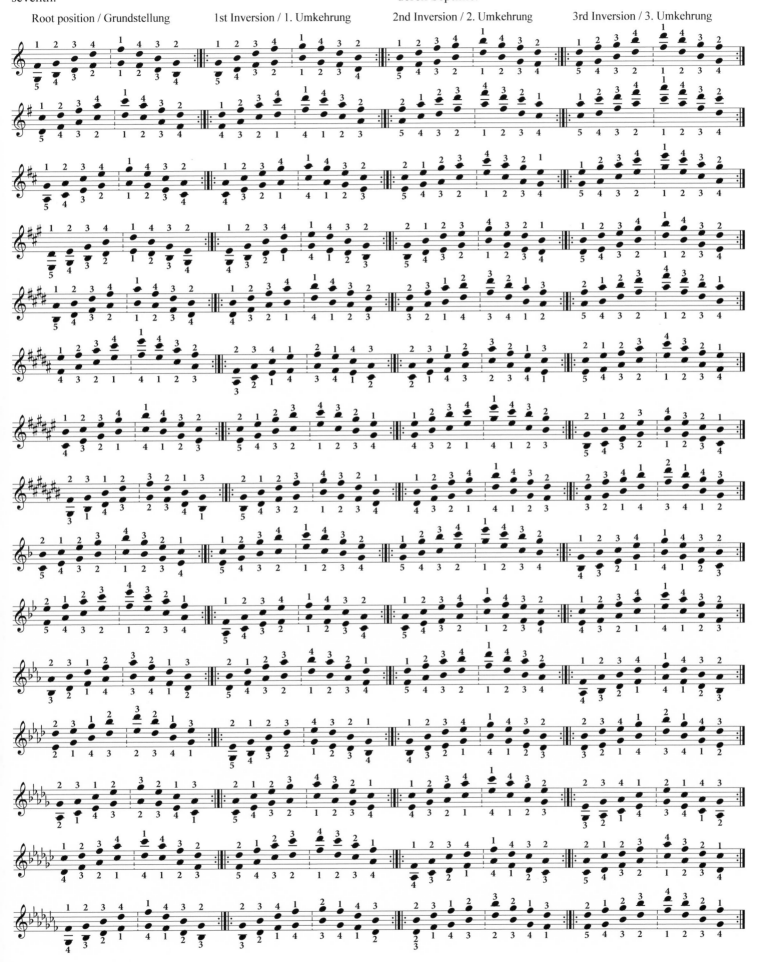

Broken chords of the diminished seventh with the octave

Gebrochene verminderte Septakkorde in Oktaven

Root position / Grundstellung   1st Inversion / 1. Umkehrung   2nd Inversion / 2. Umkehrung   3rd Inversion / 3. Umkehrung

Broken chords of the diminished seventh

The left hand commences on the leading note, the right hand on its third or on its tenth.

Gebrochene verminderte Septakkorde

Die linke Hand beginnt mit dem Leitton, die rechte Hand mit dessen Terz oder dessen Dezime.

Root position / Grundstellung   1st Inversion / 1. Umkehrung   2nd Inversion / 2. Umkehrung   3rd Inversion / 3. Umkehrung

Broken chords of the diminished seventh
The left hand commences on the leading note, the right hand with its diminished fifth.

Gebrochene verminderte Septakkorde
Die linke Hand beginnt mit dem Leitton, die rechte Hand mit dessen verminderter Quinte.

Root position / Grundstellung   1st Inversion / 1. Umkehrung   2nd Inversion / 2. Umkehrung   3rd Inversion / 3. Umkehrung

Broken chords of the diminished seventh

The left hand commences on the leading note, the right hand with its diminished seventh.

Gebrochene verminderte Septakkorde

Die linke Hand beginnt mit dem Leitton, die rechte Hand mit dessen verminderter Septime.

Root position / Grundstellung 1st Inversion / 1. Umkehrung 2nd Inversion / 2. Umkehrung 3rd Inversion / 3. Umkehrung

Broken chords of the dominant seventh
in contrary motion, commencing in unison

Gebrochene Dominant-Septakkorde
in Gegenbewegung, mit dem Einklang beginnend

Root position / Grundstellung   1st Inversion / 1. Umkehrung   2nd Inversion / 2. Umkehrung   3rd Inversion / 3. Umkehrung

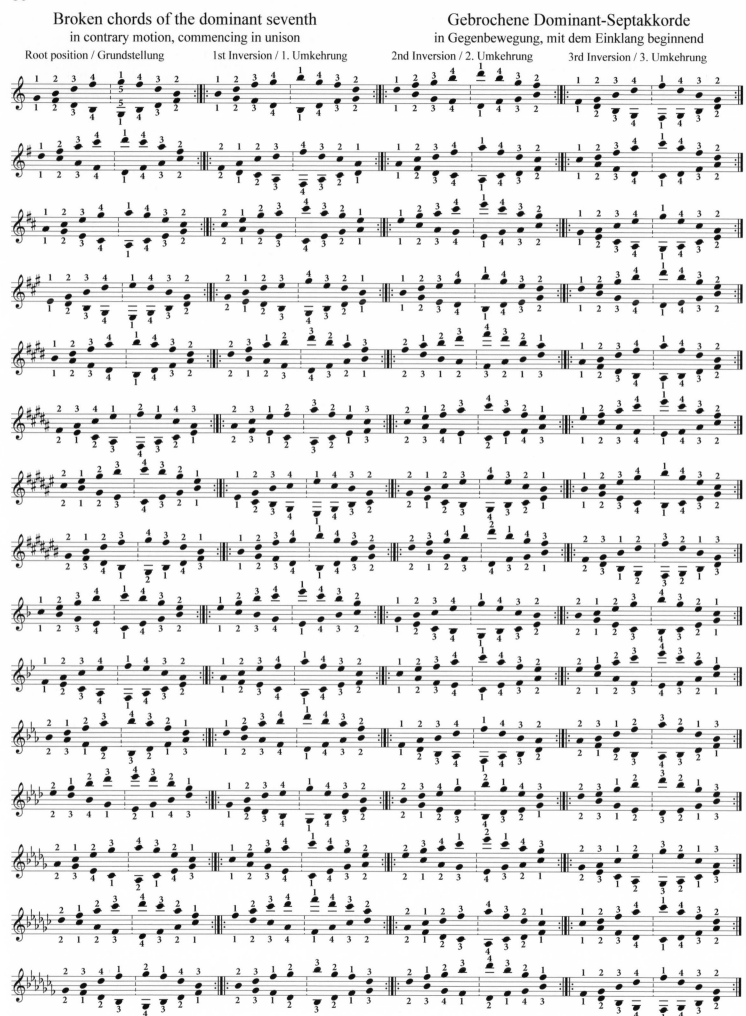

Broken chords of the diminished seventh
in contrary motion, commencing in unison

Gebrochene verminderte Septakkorde
in Gegenbewegung, mit dem Einklang beginnend

Root position / Grundstellung   1st Inversion / 1. Umkehrung   2nd Inversion / 2. Umkehrung   3rd Inversion / 3. Umkehrung

43

Melodic minor scales
ascending with the sixth and seventh of the major scale, descending with the seventh and sixth of the melodic minor scale

Melodische Molltonleitern
aufwärts mit der Sexte und der Septime der Durtonleiter, abwärts mit der Septime und der Sexte der melodischen Molltonleiter

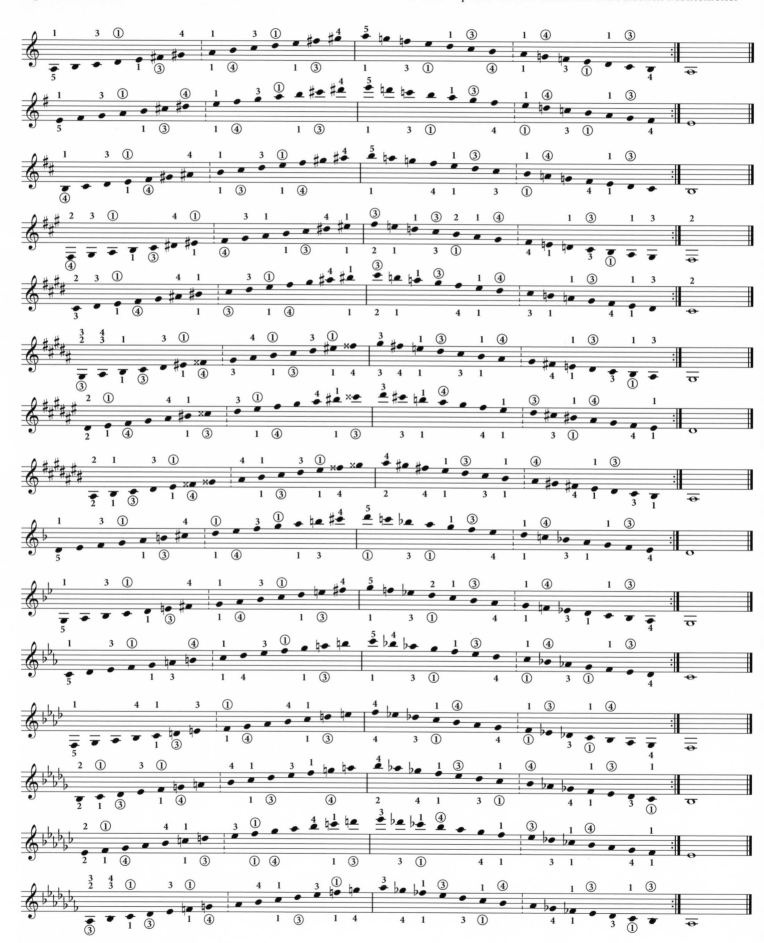

This page is left blank to save an unnecessary page turn.
Aus wendetechnischen Gründen bleibt diese Seite frei.

Third Part

Virtuose exercises to enable the pupil
to overcome the greatest technical difficulties

Dritter Teil

Virtuose Übungen zur Überwindung
der größten technischen Schwierigkeiten

44

The notes to be repeated three times without raising the hand or the wrist. As soon as the first four bars are well practised, the rest of the exercise should be studied.

Dreimalige Wiederholung jeder Note, ohne die Hand oder das Handgelenk zu heben. Wenn man die vier ersten Takte beherrscht, werden die folgenden Abschnitte ebenso geübt.

45

The consecutive notes
with 6 different fingerings

This 1st line should be practised until it is well known, the whole page can be played without stopping when the 6 first lines have been mastered. The 1st of the two tied notes to be accented.

Zwei aufeinanderfolgende Noten
mit 6 verschiedenen Fingersätzen

Das erste System so oft üben, bis es fehlerfrei beherrscht wird, danach auch mit den folgenden 5 Fingersätzen. Zuletzt wird die ganze Seite ohne Pause durchgespielt. Die jeweils erste der beiden gebundenen Noten ist zu betonen.

46

Exercise on the trill for the 5 fingers

This 1st line is to be practised until it can be played as quickly as possible, then the rest of the exercise should be practised. Care should be taken that the change to the 1st finger is performed with perfect evenness. ✳

Trillerübung für alle 5 Finger

Die beiden ersten Systeme sollten so lange geübt werden, bis das schnellstmögliche Tempo erreicht ist, erst dann wird die Übung fortgesetzt.

Besonders ist darauf zu achten, dass der Wechsel zum 1. Finger vollkommen gleichmäßig ausfällt. ✳

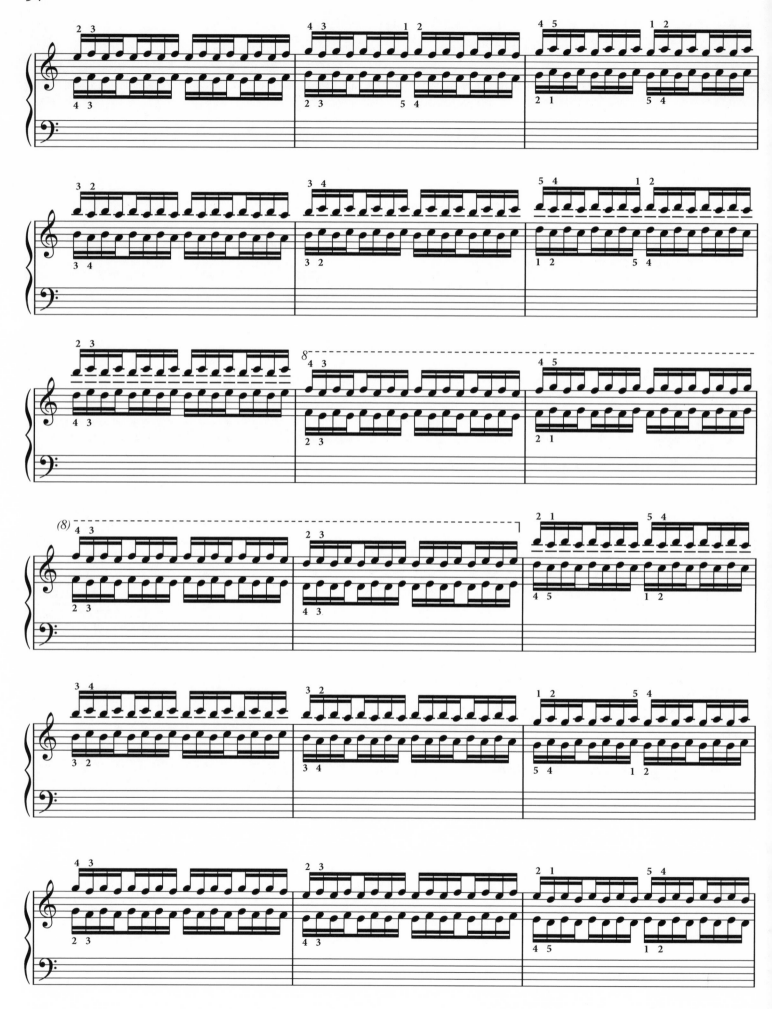

It is interesting to observe that Mozart
Es ist nicht uninteressant zu erfahren,

used this exercise for the practice of the trill.
dass Mozart diese Trillerübung mit Vorliebe benutzt hat.

Trill used by Thalberg.
Triller Thalbergs.

47

Notes repeated 4 times

In this exercise the fingers should be lifted clearly without raising the hand or wrist. Only when the 1st part is perfectly mastered, should the rest of this exercise be practised.

Viermalige Wiederholung jeder Note

Während dieser ganzen Übung die Finger sauber anheben, aber nicht die Hand oder das Handgelenk. Erst wenn man den ersten Teil perfekt beherrscht, setzt man die Übung fort.

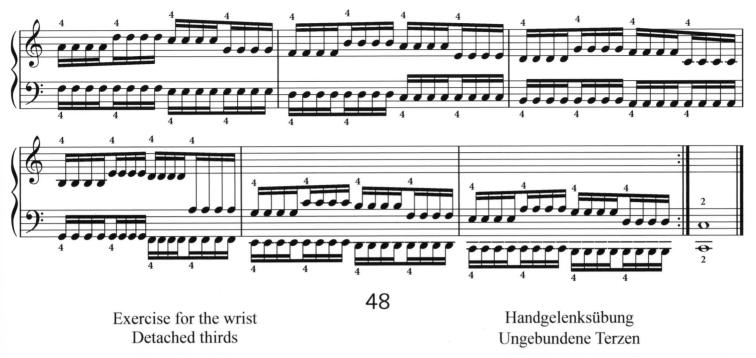

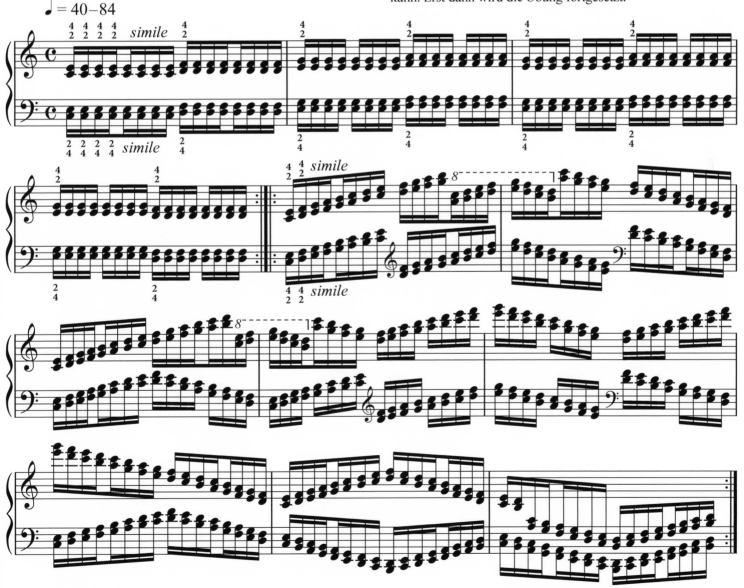

48

Exercise for the wrist
Detached thirds

Handgelenksübung
Ungebundene Terzen

The wrist should be raised at each note, the arm remaining steady
The wrists should be flexible and the fingers firm without stiffness.
The first 4 bars should be practised until they can be played easily;
then the rest of this exercise should be learned.

Die Handgelenke müssen bei jeder Note angehoben werden,
bleiben aber locker, die Arme werden nicht bewegt. Die Finger
bleiben fest, aber nicht steif. Die ersten 4 Takte werden so lange
geübt, bis man sie mit Leichtigkeit und Deutlichkeit ausführen
kann. Erst dann wird die Übung fortgesetzt.

♩ = 40–84

98

Detached Sixths

Same remarks as for the thirds.

Ungebundene Sexten

Hier gelten dieselben Bemerkungen wie bei den Terzen.

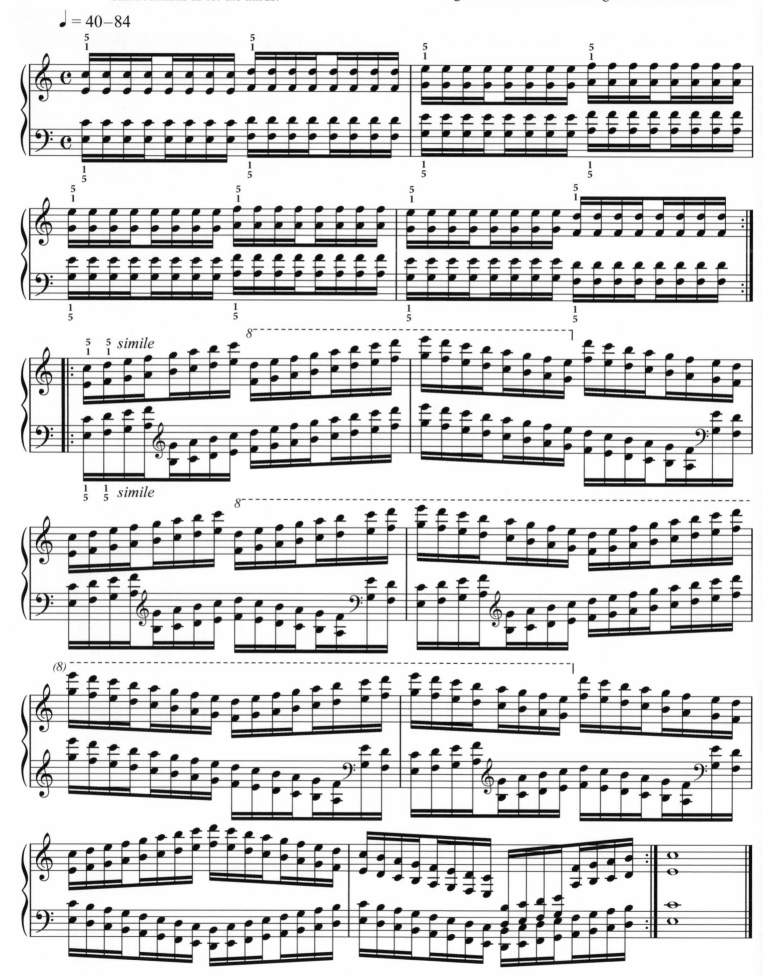

49

Exercises for stretching between the 1st and the 4th
and between the 2nd and the 5th fingers of each hand

Streckung zwischen dem 1. und 4.
sowie dem 2. und 5. Finger beider Hände

These exercises are a perfect stretching training.

Diese Übungen sind dafür ein ausgezeichnetes Training.

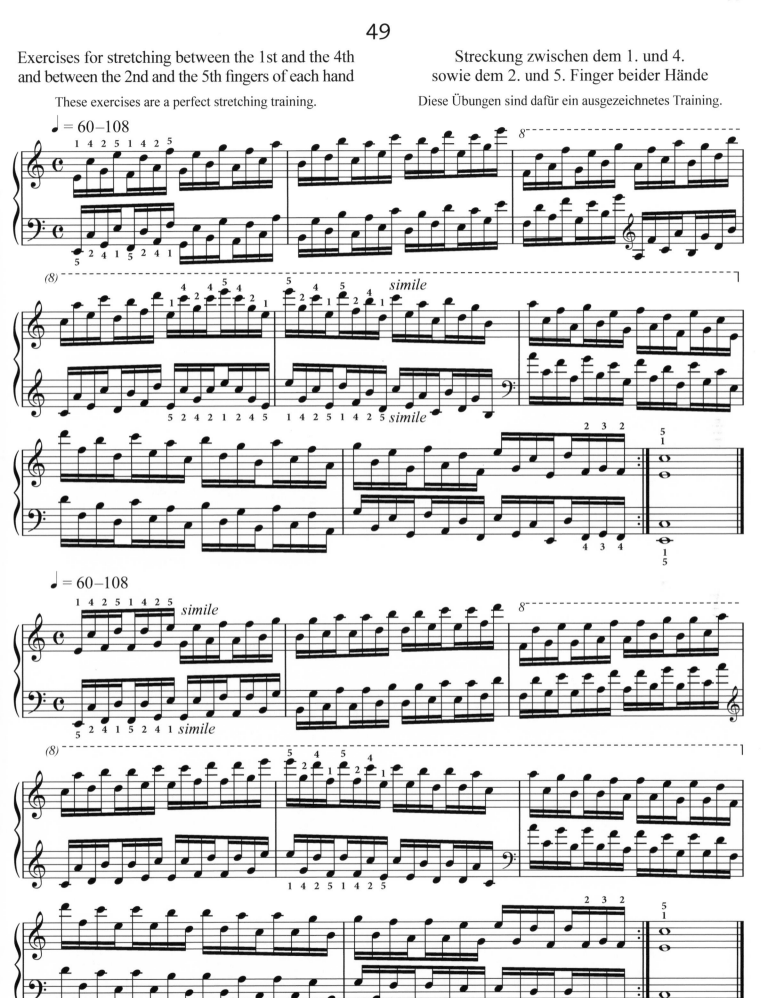

50

Runs in thirds

This exercise should be studied carefully, for thirds are used extensively in difficult music. Each note should be struck evenly and distinctly.

Terzenläufe

Diese Übung ist sorgfätig zu studieren, denn die Terzen nehmen in der schwierigeren Musikliteratur einen überaus wichtigen Platz ein. Alle Noten müssen vollkommen gleichmäßig und deutlich angeschlagen werden.

Scales in tied thirds

It is indispensable when practising the scales in thirds to play them legato. To tie the scales, the 5th finger of the right hand should be kept on one note of the third while the thumb and the 3rd finger pass over to the following third; in the left hand, the same movement is executed. We have marked in white those notes that should be held. Proceed accordingly in the following chromatic scales, and all the scales in thirds.

Tonleitern in gebundenen Terzen

Es ist unerlässlich, die Terzenskalen legato zu üben. Um sie gut miteinander zu verbinden, lässt man den 5. Finger der rechten Hand einen Moment auf der einen Terznote liegen, während man den Daumen und den 3. Finger vorbeiführt, um die nächste Terz zu spielen; mit der linken Hand lässt man ebenso den Daumen auf der entsprechenden Note ruhen, während man die gleiche Bewegung ausführt. Die Noten, die auf diese Weise gehalten werden müssen, wurden weiß gelassen. Bei den chromatischen und allen übrigen Terzenskalen wird ebenso verfahren.

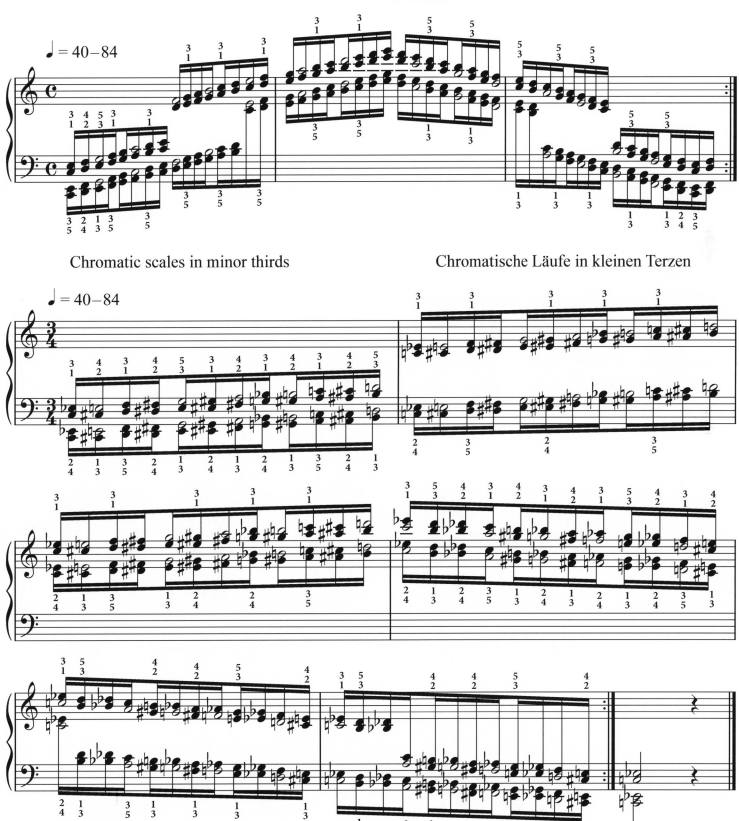

Chromatic scales in minor thirds

Chromatische Läufe in kleinen Terzen

© 2016 Schott Music GmbH & Co. KG, Mainz

51

Preparatory exercises for the scales in octaves

The wrists should be very supple, the fingers which span the octave, firm without being rigid; and those in the middle, slightly bent. These first two lines should be repeated slowly until they can be played easily and clearly; then the tempo should be increased while playing the exercise without interruption. If the wrists become tired, the tempo should be reduced until the fatigue has passed, then the former tempo can be resumed.

Vorübungen für Oktavenläufe

Das Handgelenk muss immer sehr locker bleiben, die Finger, welche die Oktave umfassen, stabil, aber nicht steif, die mittleren Finger leicht gebogen. Die beiden ersten Systeme werden zunächst in langsamem Tempo so oft wiederholt, bis sie leicht und deutlich wiedergegeben werden können. Dann wird das Tempo beschleunigt und die Übung ohne Unterbrechung fortgesetzt. Ermüden die Handgelenke, wird das Tempo verlangsamt, bis die Ermüdung verschwunden ist. Dann kann im ersten Tempo erneut begonnen werden.

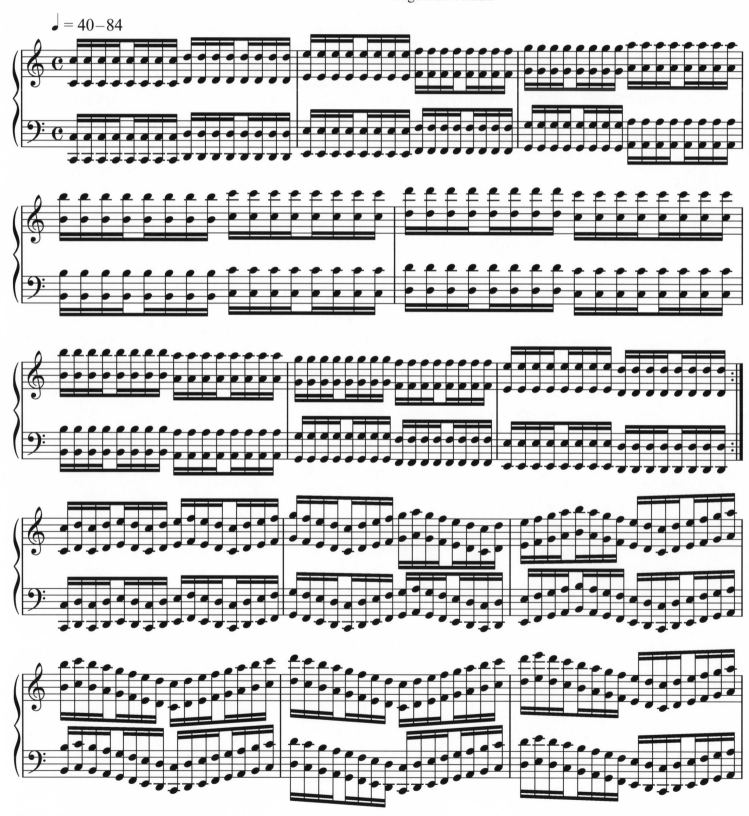

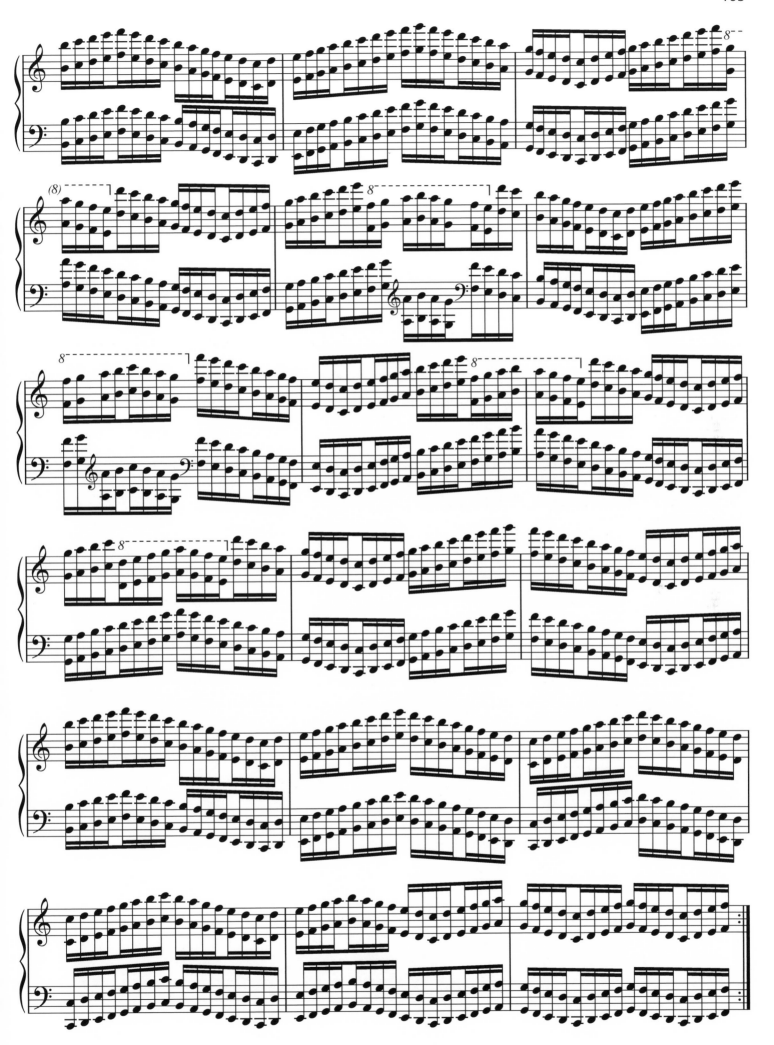

52

Scales in thirds in the most frequently used keys

Terzenläufe durch die gebräuchlichsten Tonarten

These scales should be practised with great evenness, and the ties observed. It is of the utmost importance to master them perfectly. See remarks on No. 50.

Diese Läufe müssen in perfekter Gleichmäßigkeit und Gebundenheit geübt werden, es ist überaus wichtig, sie vollkommen zu beherrschen. Siehe auch die Anmerkungen zu No. 50.

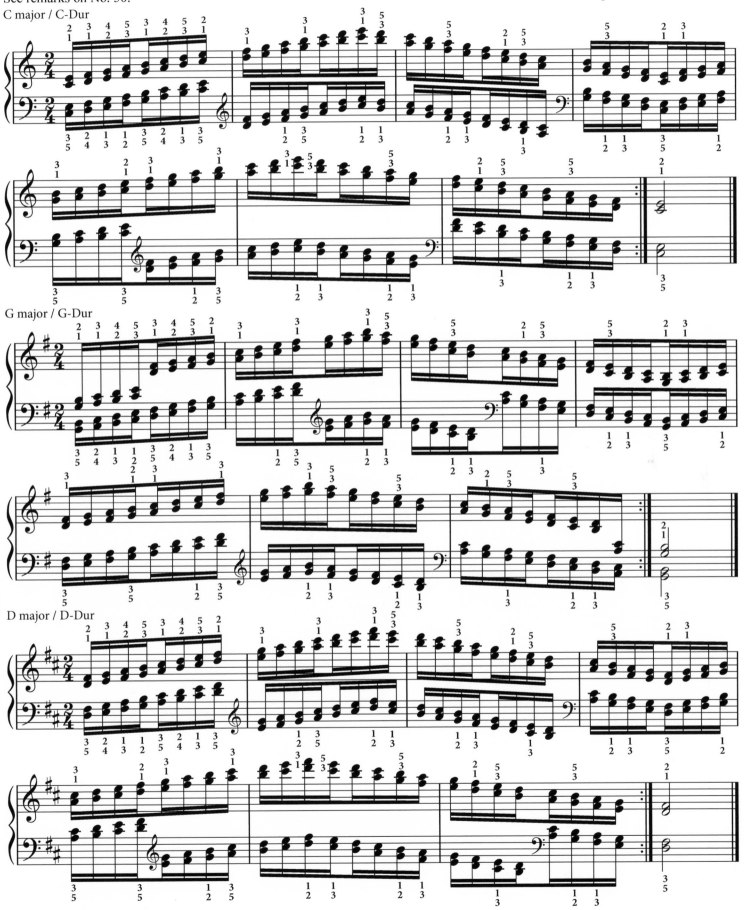

A major / A-Dur

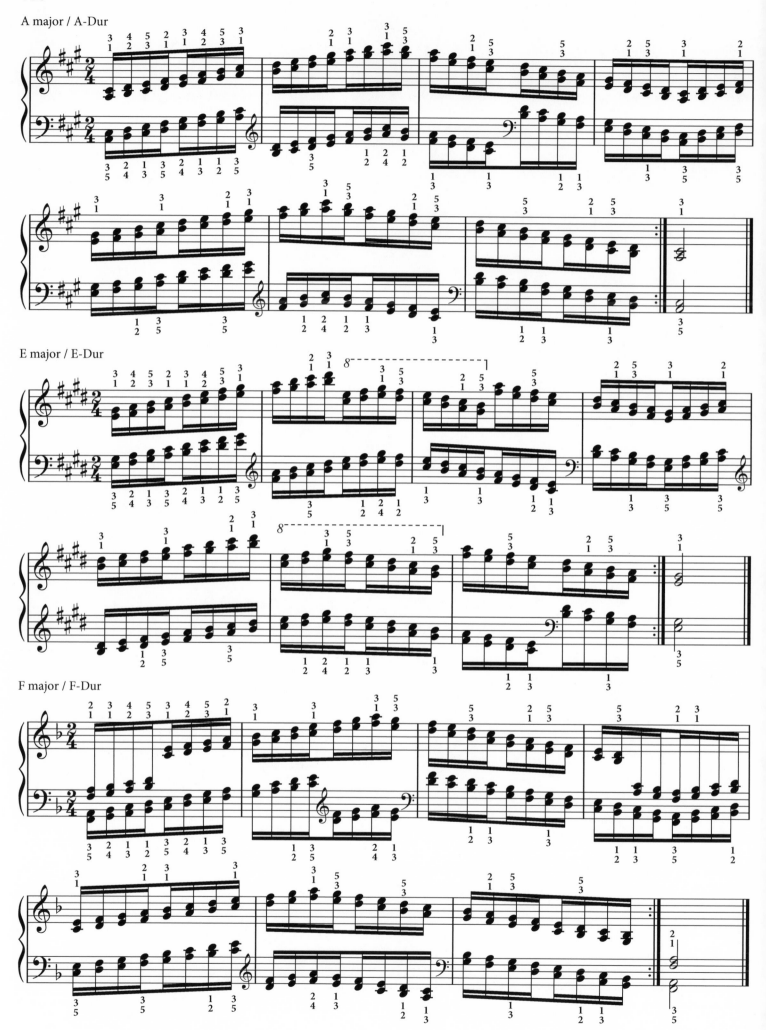

E major / E-Dur

F major / F-Dur

B♭ major / B-Dur

E♭ major / Es-Dur

A♭ major / As-Dur

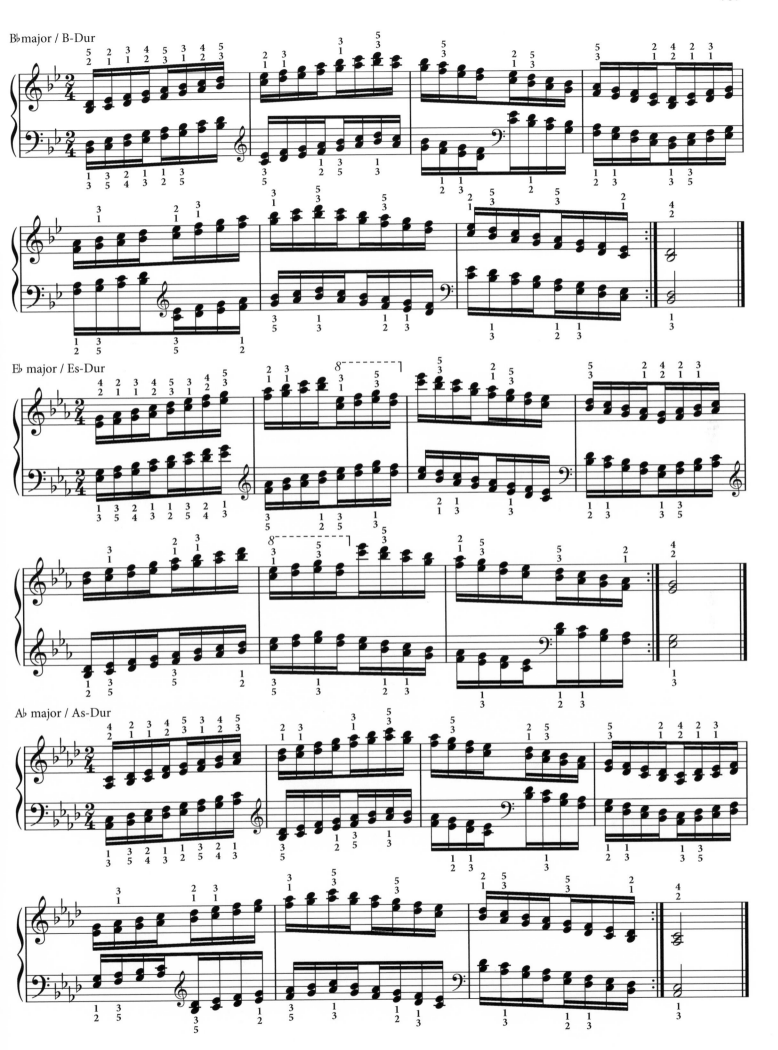

A minor / a-Moll

D minor / d-Moll

G minor / g-Moll

53

Scales in octaves in the 24 keys

Each of these scales should be practised until it can be played with ease; then the 24 scales should be played without interruption.

We cannot insist too much on the need for suppleness of the wrist; it is only thus that octaves can be played lively and forcefully, yet without rigidity. See remarks on Nos. 48 and 51.

Oktavenläufe in den 24 Tonarten

Zuerst wird jeder einzelne Lauf geübt, bis die erforderliche Leichtigkeit erreicht ist, danach werden alle 24 Läufe nacheinander ohne Unterbrechung gespielt.

Es kann nicht oft genug betont werden, wie wichtig ein leichter und lockerer Anschlag mit Hilfe des Handgelenks ist, denn das ist das einzige Mittel, die Oktaven lebhaft und energisch, aber ohne Steifheit auszuführen.

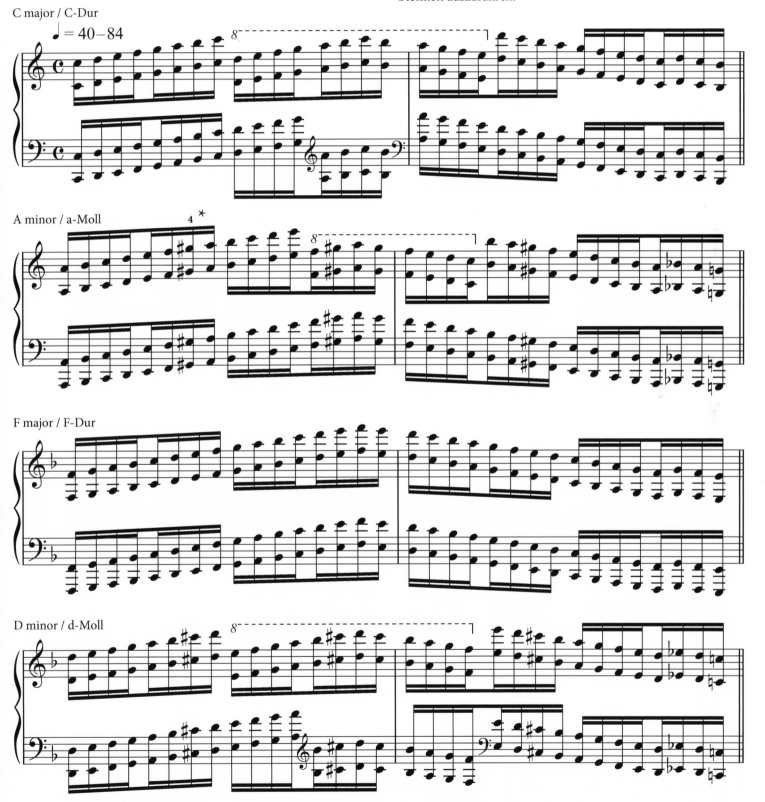

* In all the scales in octaves, the black notes should be played with the 4th finger of each hand.

* Bei allen Oktavenläufen werden die schwarzen Tasten in beiden Händen mit dem 4. Finger angeschlagen.

B♭ major / B-Dur

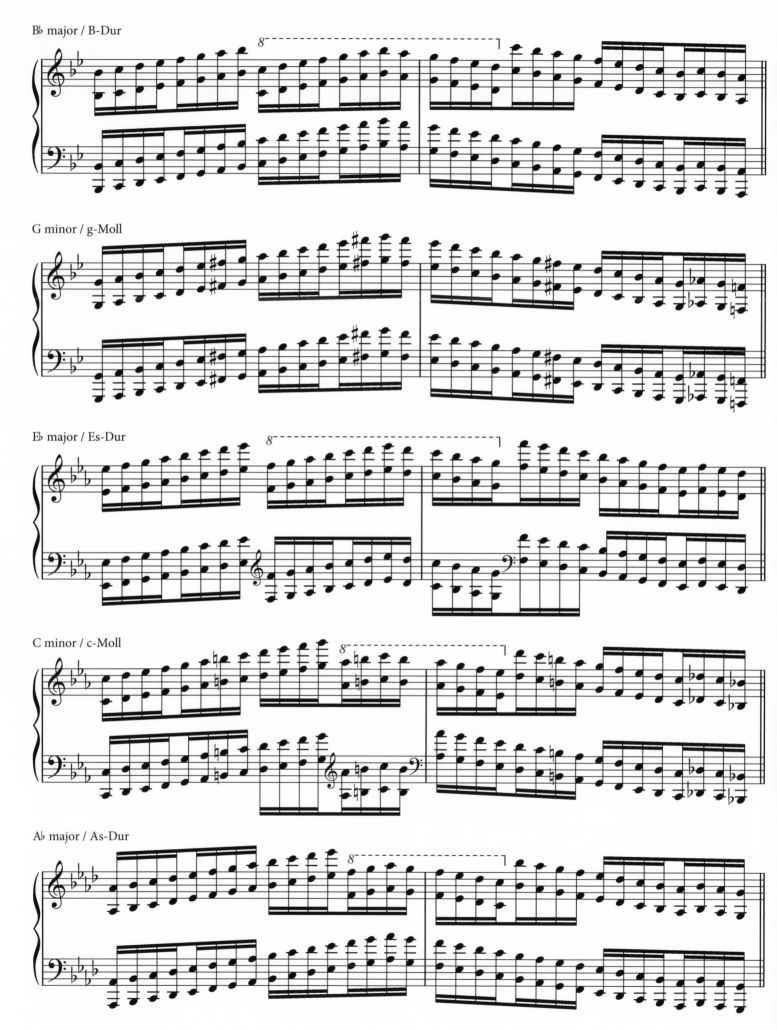

G minor / g-Moll

E♭ major / Es-Dur

C minor / c-Moll

A♭ major / As-Dur

F minor / f-Moll

Db major / Des-Dur

Bb minor / b-Moll

Gb major / Ges-Dur

Eb minor / es-Moll

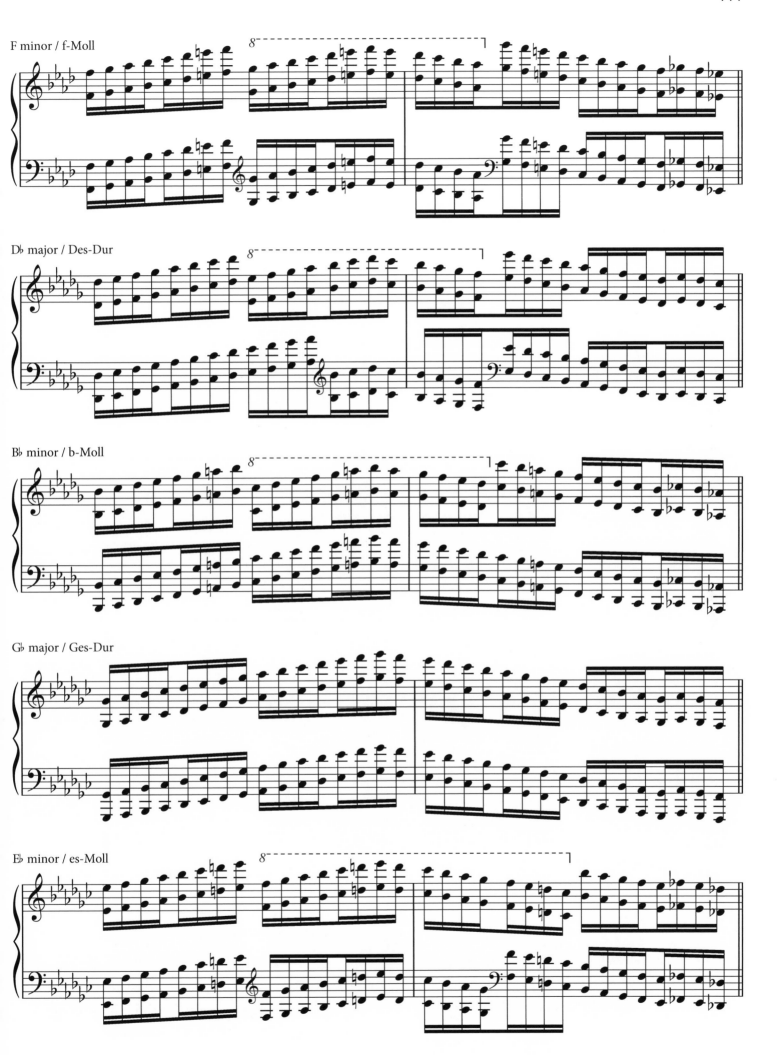

112

B major / H-Dur

G♯ minor / gis-Moll

E major / E-Dur

C♯ minor / cis-Moll

A major / A-Dur

F♯ minor / fis-Moll

D major / D-Dur

B minor / h-Moll

G major / G-Dur

E minor / e-Moll

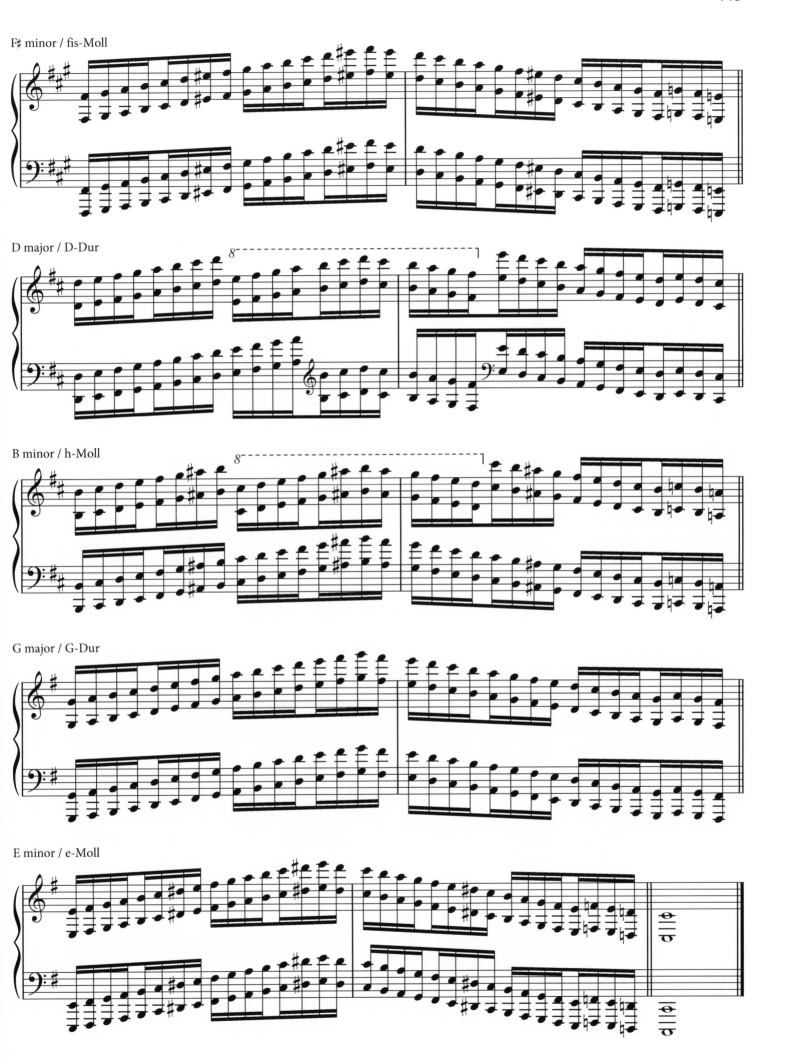

The quadruple trill in thirds for the 5 fingers

54

Vierfacher Triller in Terzen für alle 5 Finger

This exercise should be played with great evenness, striking each third very clearly.

Diese Übung soll vollkommen gleichmäßig ausgeführt werden, damit jede einzelne Terz deutlich zur Geltung kommt.

$\quad = 40–92$

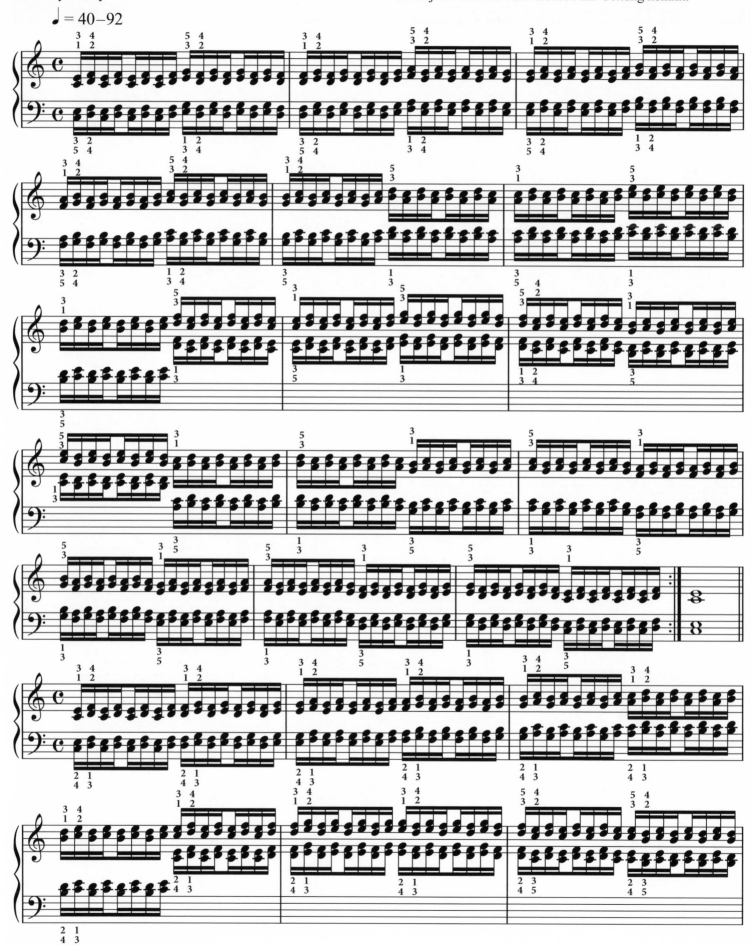

55

The triple trill (in thirds and sixths)
The same remark as for No. 54

Dreifacher Triller (Terzen und Sexten)
Die Anmerkung zu No. 54 gilt auch hier.

ben marcato

ben marcato

Fingering especially used for the quadruple trill   **Besonderer Fingersatz für den vierfachen Triller**

another fingering / anderer Fingersatz

56

Scales in broken octaves in the 24 keys   **Gebrochene Oktavenläufe in allen 24 Tonarten**

These should be played without interruption. This exercise, which is very important, prepares the wrist for the tremolo.

Diese Übung ist ohne Unterbrechung durchzuspielen. Sie bildet ein äußerst wichtiges Training der Handgelenke als Vorbereitung zum Tremolo.

♩ = 60–120

C major / C-Dur

A minor / a-Moll

F major / F-Dur

D minor / d-Moll

* Throughout this exercise, the black notes should be struck with the 4th finger of each hand.

* Bei allen Oktavengängen werden die schwarzen Tasten in jeder Hand mit dem 4. Finger angeschlagen.

B♭ major / B-Dur

G minor / g-Moll

E♭ major / Es-Dur

C minor / c-Moll

Ab major / As-Dur

F minor / f-Moll

Db major / Des-Dur

Bb minor / b-Moll

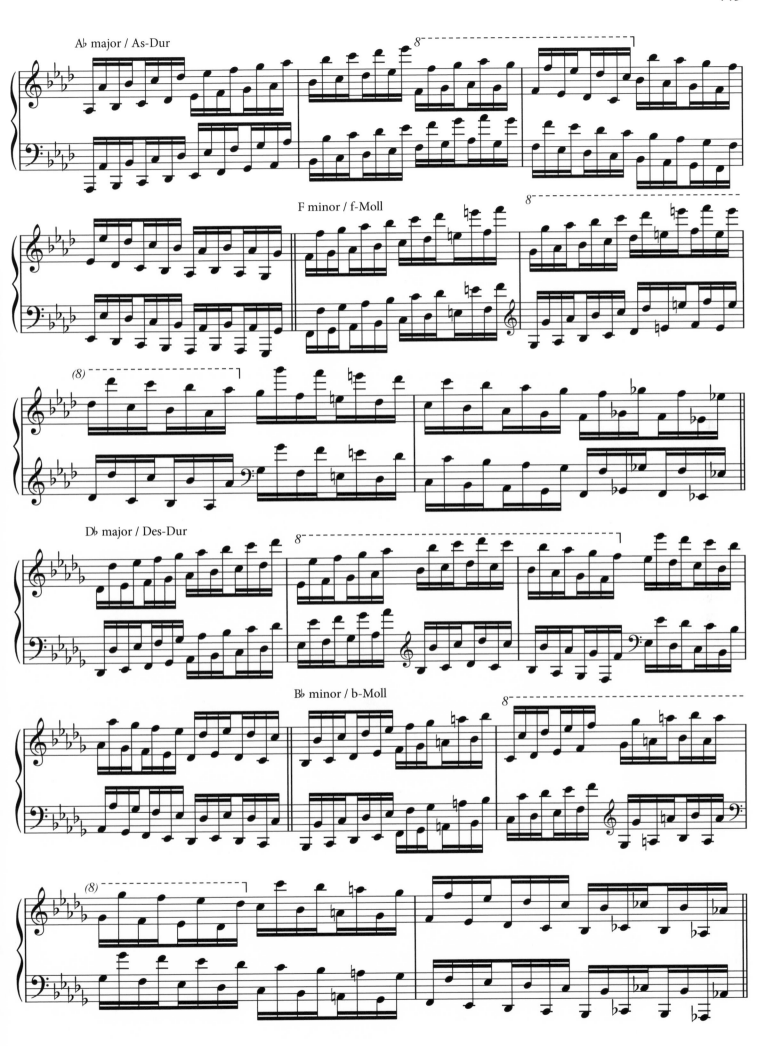

Gb major / Ges-Dur

Eb minor / es-Moll

B major / H-Dur

G# minor / gis-Moll

E major / E-Dur

C♯ minor / cis-Moll

A major / A-Dur

F♯ minor / fis-Moll

D major / D-Dur

B minor / h-Moll

G major / G-Dur

E minor / e-Moll

This page is left blank to save an unnecessary page turn.
Aus wendetechnischen Gründen bleibt diese Seite frei.

57

Arpeggios in broken octaves in 24 keys

The 1st arpeggio in C should first be practised; and only when it can be played easily, clearly, and with perfect freedom of the wrist should the pupil proceed to the following one in A minor.

The 24 arpeggios should be studied in this way before playing them without interruption.

Gebrochene Oktavenarpeggien in allen 24 Tonarten

Mit dem ersten Arpeggio in C-Dur beginnen und erst dann zu a-Moll übergehen, wenn es mit völlig freiem Handgelenk sauber und deutlich gespielt werden kann. In dieser Weise alle 24 Arpeggi einzeln üben, bevor man sie ohne Unterbrechung durchspielt.

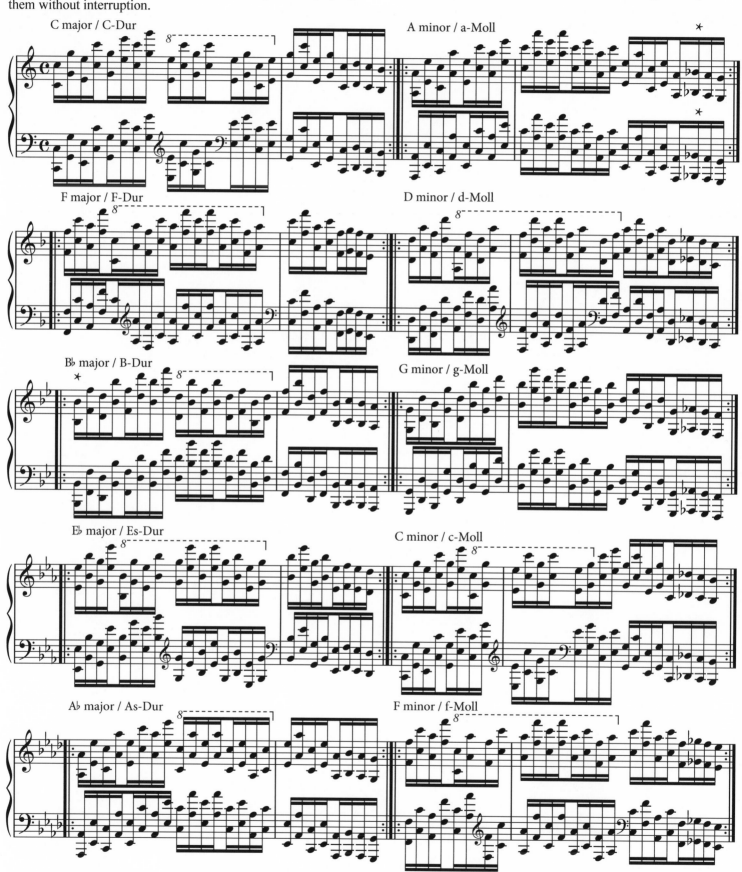

* Throughout this exercise, the black notes should be struck with the 4th finger of each hand.

* Bei allen diesen Übungen werden die schwarzen Tasten in beiden Händen mit dem 4. Finger angeschlagen.

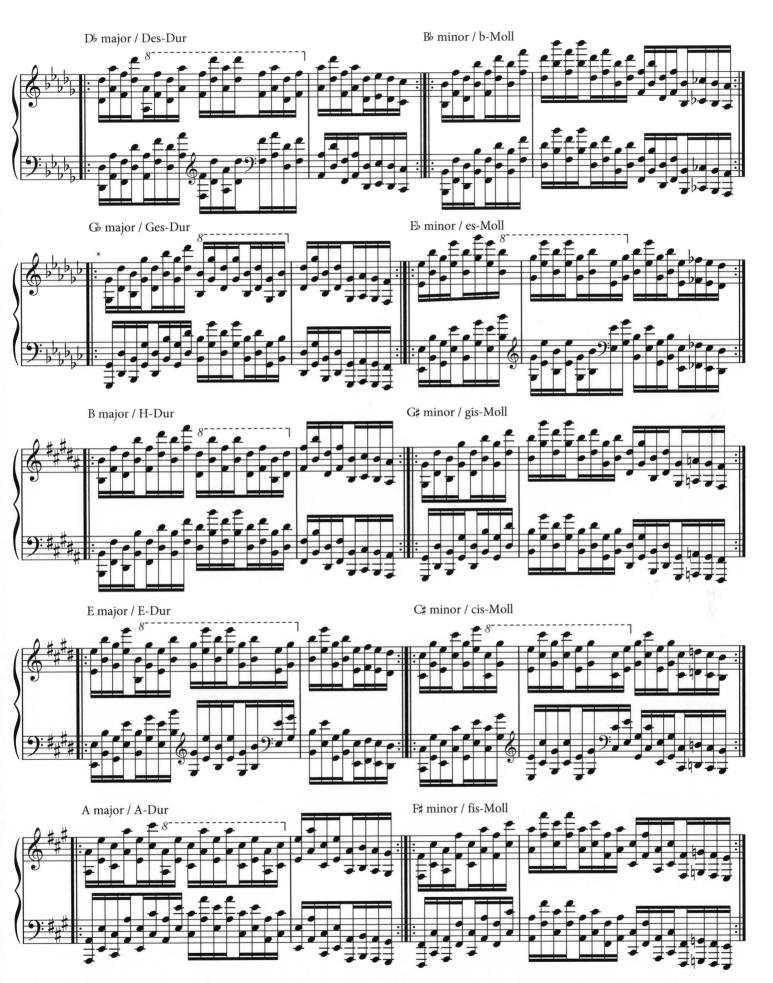

Db major / Des-Dur

Bb minor / b-Moll

Gb major / Ges-Dur

Eb minor / es-Moll

B major / H-Dur

G# minor / gis-Moll

E major / E-Dur

C# minor / cis-Moll

A major / A-Dur

F# minor / fis-Moll

* This arpeggios and the following in Eb minor being played entirely on black keys, they can be struck either with the 4th or the 5th finger.

* Da dieses und das Arpeggio in es-Moll ausschließlich auf schwarzen Tasten gespielt werden, ist es gleichgültig, ob man sie mit dem 4. oder mit dem 5. Finger anschlägt.

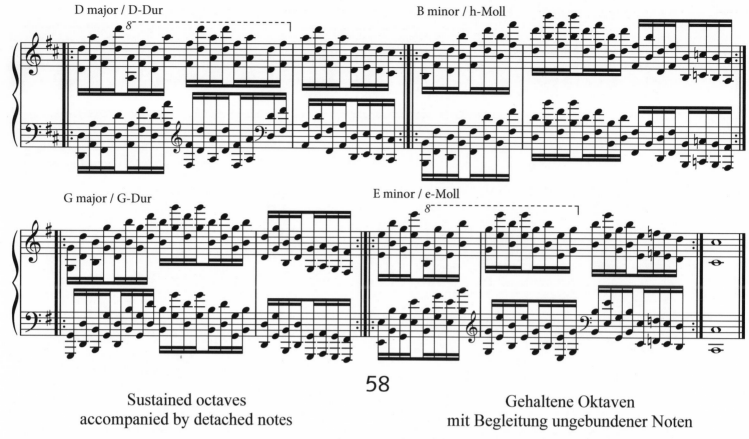

D major / D-Dur   B minor / h-Moll

G major / G-Dur   E minor / e-Moll

58

<table>
<tr><td>

Sustained octaves
accompanied by detached notes

The octaves should be played vigorously without moving the wrists; and the intermediate semiquaver groups should be played lively and distinctly.

</td><td>

Gehaltene Oktaven
mit Begleitung ungebundener Noten

Die Oktaven werden mit großer Kraft, aber ohne Beteiligung des Handgelenks angeschlagen, während die dazwischenliegenden Sechzehntelgruppen lebhaft und deutlich akzentuiert gespielt werden müssen.

</td></tr>
</table>

59

Quadruple trill in sixths

Exercise for stretching between the thumb and 4th finger, and the 2nd and 5th fingers of each hand.

No movement of the hand or wrist should be made while playing this exercise.

Vierfacher Triller, notiert in Sexten

Übung für die Streckung zwischen dem 1. und 4. und dem 2. und 5. Finger beider Hände. Sie ist ohne Bewegung der Hand oder des Handgelenks auszuführen.

♩ = 40–84

This bar is to be repeated 4 times
Diesen Takt 4-mal wiederholen

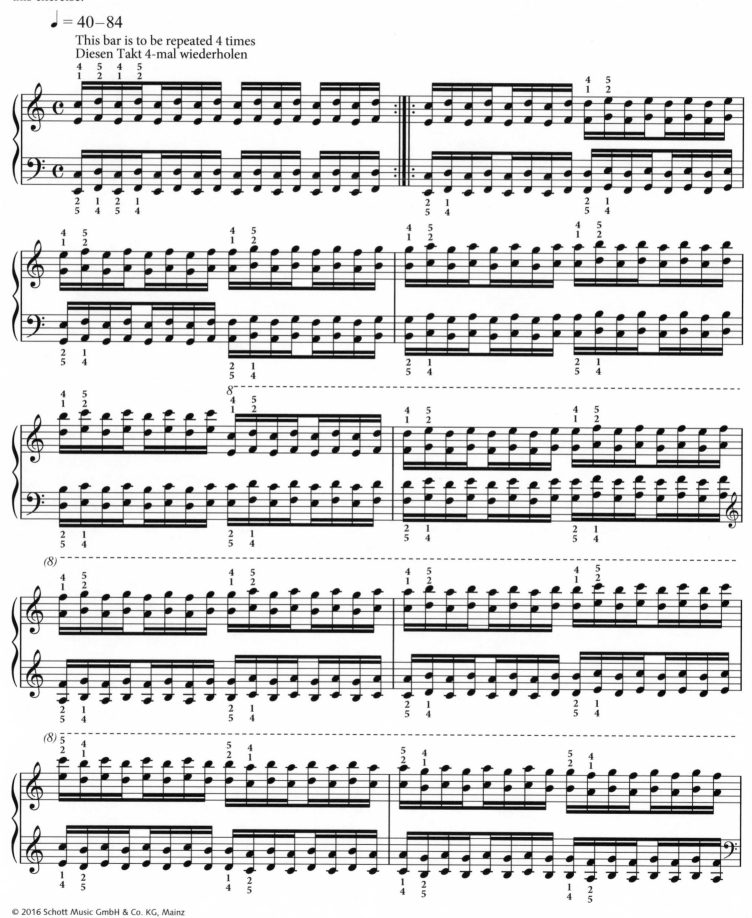

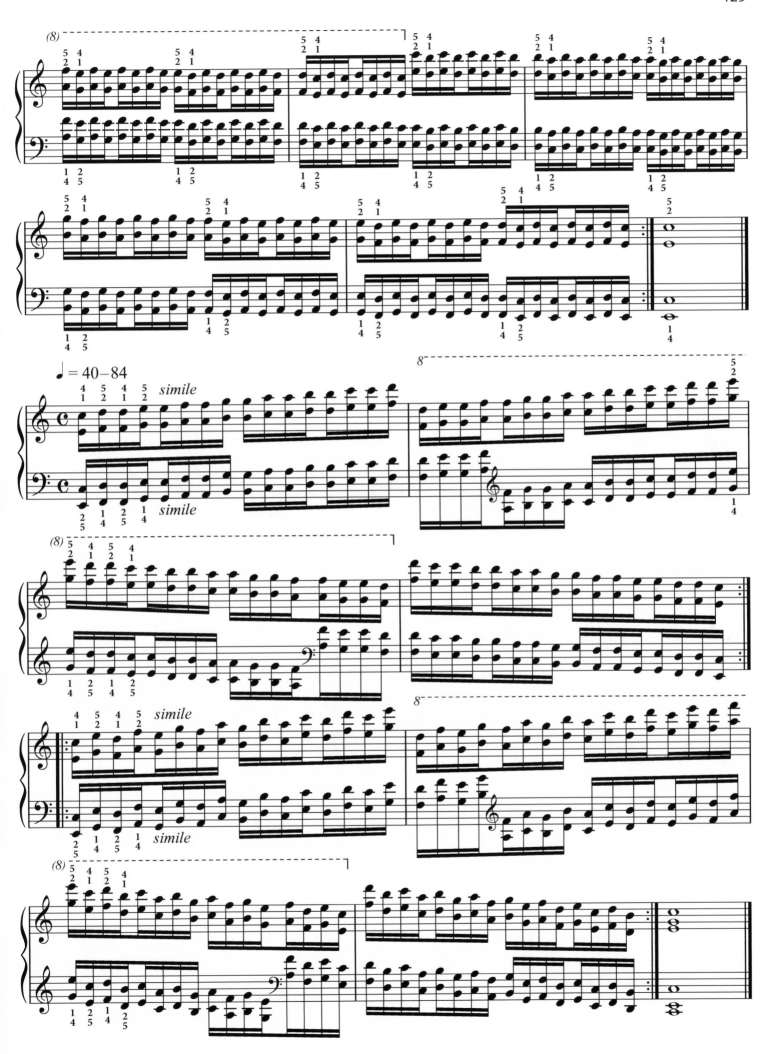

60

The tremolo

To play the tremolo properly, it should be executed with the rapidity of a drum roll. It should be practised slowly to begin with: the speed should be gradually increased until it reaches 72. Finally the speed should be further increased by movements of the wrist until it resembles the roll of a drum. This study is long and difficult, but the excellence of the result obtained will compensate the pianist for the trouble and fatigue undergone in its pursuit.

Das Tremolo

Soll ein Tremolo wirkungsvoll sein, muss es die Geschwindigkeit eines Paukenwirbels besitzen. Zuerst wird langsam geübt, dann beschleunigt, bis das Tempo 72 erreicht ist. Danach wird das Tempo nochmals erhöht, indem das Handgelenk locker hin und her bewegt wird, bis die Geschwindigkeit eines Paukenwirbels erreicht ist. Diese Übung erfordert viel Zeit und ist extrem schwierig, aber das letztendlich erreichte Resultat wird den Pianisten für alle Mühe entschädigen.

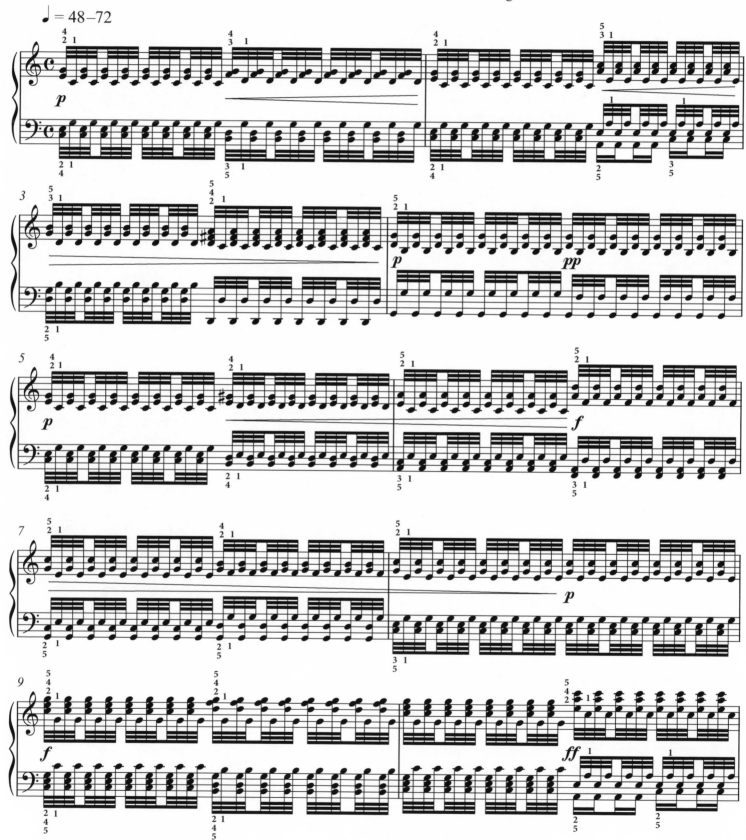

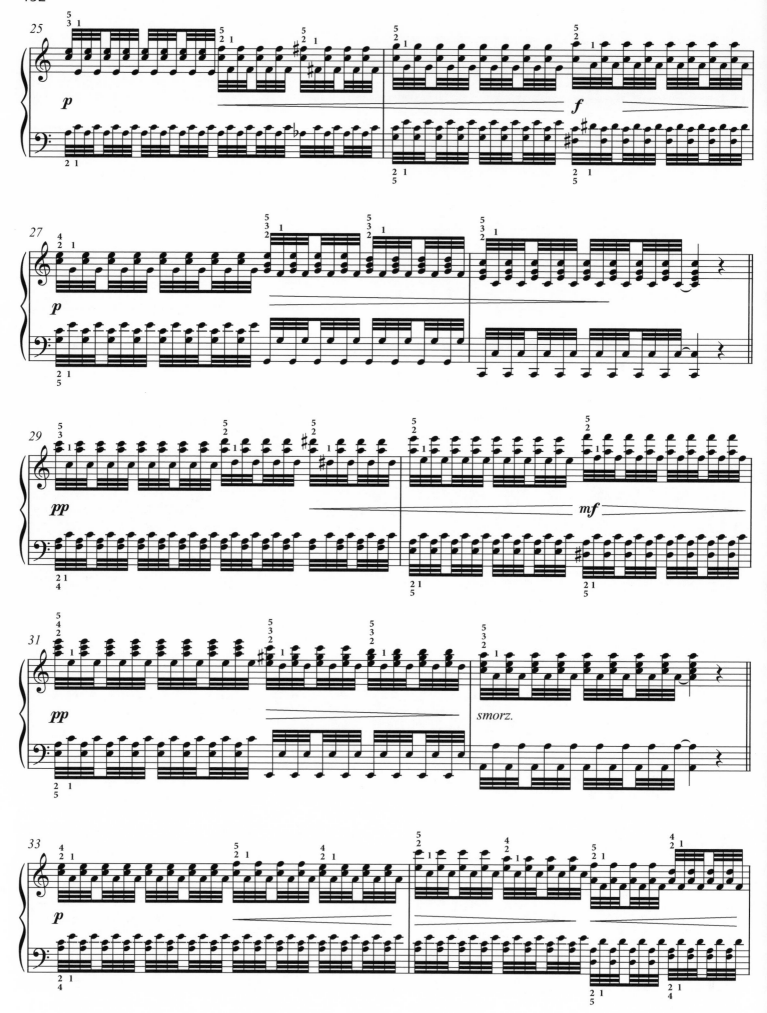

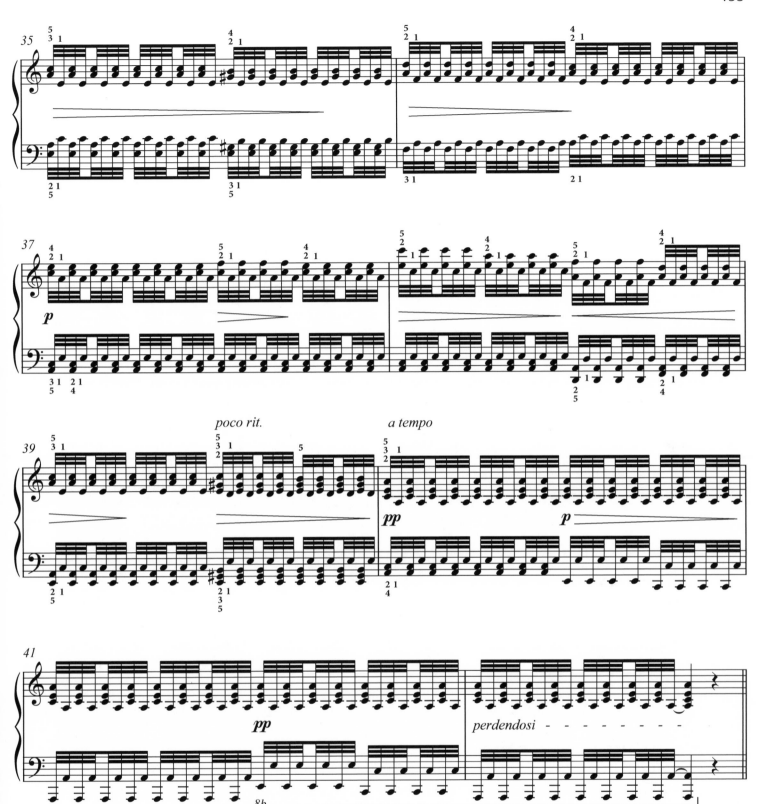

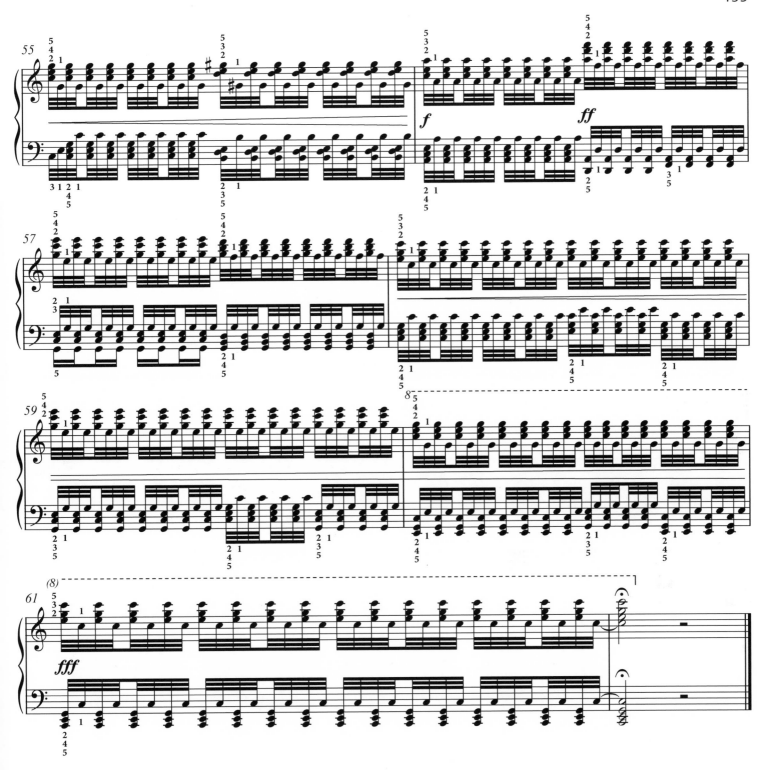

Conclusion

Now that the pupil has studied this volume, he is acquainted with the greater part of the mechanical difficulties; but if he wishes to obtain the reward of his work and become a true artist, he should play this whole book for a certain time every day; only then will these great difficulties become familiar to him. A minimum of one hour is required to play the whole of this work, this is very little trouble in comparison with the immense advantages which will result from it. The greatest artists are obliged to play exercises several hours every day, to preserve their technique. We can not therefore be accused of exaggeration when we ask that these studies be played once every day in order to become a true artist.

Zum Abschluss

Wenn der Schüler diesen ganzen Band durchgearbeitet hat, kennt er die größten Schwierigkeiten der Technik. Wenn er aber die Früchte seiner Mühen wirklich ernten und ein echter Virtuose werden will, so muss er während einer gewissen Zeit dieses Buch alle Tage von Anfang bis Ende durchspielen; erst dann werden ihm die großen Schwierigkeiten wirklich vertraut sein. Um das ganze Werk durchzuspielen, ist mindestens eine Stunde erforderlich. Das ist aber nur wenig Arbeit im Vergleich zu den ungeheuren Vorteilen, die sich daraus ergeben. Die größten Virtuosen müssen gewisse Übungen täglich während mehrerer Stunden wiederholen, um ihre Technik frisch zu erhalten. Es ist also nicht übertrieben zu betonen, dass diese Übungen täglich gespielt werden müssen, wenn größtmögliches Können erreicht werden soll.